M000024805

LEADING THE EDGE OF CHANGE

LEADING THE EDGE OF CHANGE

Building Individual and Organizational Capacity
for the Evolving Nature of Change

John L. Bennett

PAW
PRINT
PRESS

Mooresville, North Carolina

Copyright 2000. All Rights Reserved

LEADING THE EDGE OF CHANGE

COPYRIGHT
2000 by John L. Bennett. All rights reserved.

PUBLISHED BY
Paw Print Press

No part of this publication may be reproduced, stored in a retrieval system or transmitted in any form or by any means, electronic, mechanical, photocopying, recording, scanning or otherwise, except as permitted under Sections 107 or 108 of the 1976 United States Copyright Act, without either the prior written permission of the Publisher. Requests to the Publisher for permission should be addressed to Paw Print Press, P.O. Box 3816, Mooresville, NC 28117-3816.

This publication is designed to provide accurate and authoritative information in regard to the subject matter covered. It is sold with the understanding that the publisher is not engaged in rendering professional services. If professional advice or other expert assistance is required, the services of a competent professional person should be sought. This book is printed on acid-free paper.

ART DIRECTION & DESIGN
Eric Johnson

LIBRARY OF CONGRESS CATALOGING-IN-PUBLICATION DATA
Bennett, John L.
    Leading the edge of change: building individual and organizational capacity for the evolving nature of change / John L Bennett. --Mooresville, NC : Paw Print Press, c2000.
        p. cm.
    ISBN 0-9678323-0-6
        1. Organizational change. 2. Management
    I. Title
HD58.8 .B462 2000   99-68955
658.4/06--dc21   CIP

ISBN
ISBN 0-9678323-0-6

WHAT OTHERS HAVE TO SAY ABOUT THIS BOOK

"The winds of change are blowing furiously through the corporate world. This book will help you navigate these winds to your greatest advantage. If your goal is to capitalize on change opportunities, John provides the principles, the plan, and the motivation."
—Tom Leger, President; Novitec

"Change Happens. Challenge Happens. Setbacks Happen. In this book John Bennett gives readers exceptional tools to transform themselves and their organizations. Read it; use it; follow it! You'll be glad you did!"—Willie Jolly, Best-selling author of *A Setback Is a Setup for a Comeback* and *It Only Takes a Minute To Change Your Life!*

"The next best thing to having this perceptive guy lead your change project is to learn his practical approach and lead the change process yourself...If you're not involved in a change, for God's sake don't read this book, because you'll be all dressed up with nowhere to go!"—Daniel Connor, President/CEO, Blood Systems, Inc.

"This is one of the most comprehensive books on the subject of change available today and a must-read to thrive in a rapidly changing environment."—David Greenberg, CSP, author of *Thank God It's Monday! Designing a Life You Love Beyond the Weekend* and *Simply Speaking*

"This practical book, written with wisdom and from experience, will nourish your mind and nurture your soul—and prepare you to embrace change with competence and confidence."—Nido R. Qubein, Chairman, Creative Services, Inc.

"Master trainer, John Bennett, has masterfully woven the insight you need to build yourself and your team to the cutting edge of change. John gives you the master's tools to lead that change."—Robert J. Danzig, Former President, Hearst Newspapers

"...loved meeting Granny and Maggie...They make what could be a difficult subject fun...I found myself rooting for Maggie and wanting to be adopted by Granny!"—T. Scott Gross, Author, *Borrowed Dreams*

"John Bennett's book is a prime primer for the neophyte and a solid guide for the seasoned. Well done!—Michael H. Mescon, Ph.D., Founder and Chairman, The Mescon Group

"The author does an excellent job of developing a logical and practical framework for change leadership. The points about teamwork and team building are presented very clearly."—A. Max Lennon, President, Mars Hill College

"...offers a valuable message to address the common dilemmas facing today's business community thus allowing the reader to stay one step ahead of his/her competition... It is a very readable book that hits the mark with practical suggestions for every business."—Tom Galyon, President and CEO, Greater Lansing Convention & Visitors Bureau

This book is dedicated to the life,
death, and living memory of Jim Wolf.
I continue to be blessed by his life.

CONTENTS

PREFACE

There are three certainties in today's world: death, taxes, and change. While we have limited control over death and taxes, fortunately change can be harnessed and turned into a powerful force that will propel you and your organization toward an exciting, new, uncharted course to growth and excellence.

The intention of this book is to help you and your organization prepare for, improve through, and excel at change by helping you understand the nature of change and how to increase your overall ability to meet the challenges of change.

I offer it as a set of thoughts and tools based on my experience as a participant in, leader of, and consultant to change efforts in a variety of industries. It is my intent to create a practical, easy-to-use guide to help you navigate through change. Certainly there is much to be said about change and how to lead it, but this book is about building sufficient capacity to "make it" through the turbulence of change.

By capacity I mean the ability to receive, contain, and absorb change and the ability to adapt in a positive manner.

This book has four major parts in which we examine change and our responses to it; the way to improve our individual ability to change; the organizational components necessary for successful change; and a general overview of change as it affects us. You'll find that this book is organized for ease of use so that you will be able to use it as a reference and workbook every time you are confronted with change.

How much change are you able to receive, absorb, contain?

In Part I we will explore the nature of change and how we respond to it. We focus on the nature of change by defining change, its prevalence, and the various types of change we are likely to encounter in our everyday world. We'll also discuss the different types of responses to change that individuals and organizations display.

Part II is designed to provide a framework for improving individual capacity for ever-present change. Here you will learn about resilience (our capacity for responding to change), and the five ingredients necessary to improve our ability to bounce back in the face of adversity. You'll also find a practical work tool for developing actions to support change capacity-building.

Increase your capacity and lead the way...

In Part III you will explore three organizational components that play a significant role in the successful implementation of change. While there are many key ingredients, experience indicates that these three important components are often less well developed, or do not receive adequate priority during change efforts.

Next you will consider the role of leadership in change by defining leadership, outlining the importance of leadership during change, and detailing how effective leadership can improve success during change.

The importance of teamwork during change will be explored. You will outline an approach for focusing teams and define several team behaviors, then you will also discuss the importance of focusing on clear project plans and managing actions.

Finally, you will explore the importance of communication, provide a method for determining the appropriate key messages for key targets, then illustrate the need to communicate to a variety of audiences in a variety of ways.

Upon finishing this book, you will learn that to produce the desired results you must understand human reactions to change; you must have the right leader working with the right people focusing on the right tasks; and, you must have effective internal and external communication.

Most importantly you will learn that you can change. You can increase your capacity to change. You can increase your capacity to help others change. You can increase your ability to guide your organizations through change. You can change and grow strong.

The time for change is now...

ACKNOWLEDGEMENTS

Writing a book has been related to giving birth. Whether or not this is accurate can be debated. This book would not be possible without the support, encouragement, and participation of many others. Through the years I have been blessed with opportunities to grow, develop, and learn through a variety of experiences. The freedom to do so has been of tremendous value. This work would not be possible without many of those experiences, some of which were self–created-all of which were a part of life's lessons.

I would like to acknowledge my parents, Bill and Allene, who have supported and attempted to guide me for more than forty years. My sister, Nancy, continues to be an inspiration for growth, individualism, and unconditional love.

Others for whom I am grateful are numerous. The risk of listing anyone by name is the likelihood of omitting someone. So, I will apologize in advance and accept responsibility for any such errors. For inspiration and leaps in growth: H.E. Buddin, Hugh Meyers, Pat Carlyle, Bill Hughey, and Sarah Saeger.

Many thanks to those for whom and with whom I have been fortunate to work. I hope the learning never stops.

A special debt of gratitude is due to the late Ned Herrmann and his team at Herrmann International for granting permission to use their material.

For specific support in creating this book, I am grateful for creative writing, re-writing, and editing support from Cathy Oblin. Without her hard work, dedication, talent, and patience I do not believe this book would be possible. Joe Schubert was kind enough to review several drafts and provide encouraging advice. And, Eric Johnson— thank you for reminding me over and over that this could be done, and for putting up with me and for being so creative.

And, of course, Granny and Maggie.

INTRODUCTION

One need not look far to see that change is everywhere. In fact, the speed, complexity, and volume of change are increasing as you are reading this.

Sometimes it seems the changes come so quickly that we barely have time to assimilate one before the next one comes. We struggle to cope. Change impacts our intellect, emotions, bodies, and spirits. In the face of change, we struggle to maintain relationships, do the work we've been doing, and attempt to communicate with those around us—anything to establish stability and normalcy.

Leading the Edge of Change is about working and growing through change rather than just coping with it. It is about developing the capacity to survive, and then thrive during the turbulent winds of change we encounter every day. While giving practical solutions to the everyday and the unusual, *Leading the Edge of Change* will provide you with the essential knowledge you need about the nature of change and how individuals and organizations respond.

As an international consultant to business, government, education, and not-for-profit organizations, I have drawn from these arenas to provide examples of how to build the capacity to thrive by building resilience (increasing capacity) for change. This book was written to provide practical information and tools to help build effective change through leadership, teamwork, project and action planning, and the critical element of communication.

NATURE AND RESPONSE TO CHANGE

In Part I we examine the nature of change and how our response to change impacts our ability to cope with it. We will look at the types of change we encounter in our everyday lives and our typical responses to these changes. We will discuss danger versus opportunity; endings and beginnings; the phases of change; and the stages of change acceptance. We will also learn about the Change Style Indicator (CSI), a handy assessment tool designed to measure your individual style in approaching change and dealing with situations involving change.

1 | The Nature of Change

"Change is not made without inconvenience...even from worse to better."
—Richard Hooker

"It's hard for me to get used to these changing times. I remember when air was clean and sex was dirty."
—George Burns

I never realized how much I learned about change and resiliency from my grandmother until I sat down to write this book. That's when it occurred to me that those delightful summer vacations spent at Granny's home in the balmy South were actually a sort of summer school of life, and I was having so much fun learning, I didn't have a clue.

When it came to change, you could count on Granny to know all about it. To hear her talk about those model T's, those sputniks, and those wild computers, you'd think she'd seen everything. And, at her age (she was born at the turn of the 20th century) she probably did.

Actually if it wasn't for Granny's belief that in order to stay young you had to surround yourself with good, substantial food, new ideas, and young people, I wouldn't have met Maggie.

Maggie was the great-granddaughter of Granny's neighbor. According to Granny, Maggie had been working for the same corporation since she graduated from business school with her masters degree, but now she was on the verge of quitting because she couldn't adjust to all the changes that were going on around her. Of course, Granny didn't want to meddle, but since I seemed to know all about that stuff, maybe I could drop over and talk to Maggie sometime.

I did. And we talked. It seemed that Maggie's corporation was going through a major reorganization. Her position was being re-created which meant she would have to get further training. Maggie knew she was an intelligent woman, so she couldn't figure out why she was having a hard time with it. She was trying to do her best to keep a stiff upper lip, but it seemed the harder she tried the more she was spinning her wheels.

"What's going on John?" she asked. "I try to go with the program. I really do. Everything seemed to be going okay as it was, then they do this. It's absolutely frustrating. I don't want to quit, but I just can't. It just doesn't feel right."

As our conversation continued, it became more evident that Maggie, like most people, especially those with her level of experience, didn't have an understanding of the dynamics and complexity of change. This is where our mentor/student relationship began.

✳ ✳ ✳

What exactly is this thing called change and why does it happen? And why don't we like it?

By definition, change is to make different. Change is caused when there is a shift in actions that produce a different result. Change occurs when there is a disruption in the balance between our capabilities (ability and willingness) and challenges (opportunities and dangers) (Darryl R. Conner, 1992).

It sounds simple enough. On the one hand, we confront challenges in our personal and organizational lives on a regular basis. They come in the form of opportunities and dangers. The dangers are the events, situations, people, and issues that we want and/or possibly need to avoid. If, for example, the building you are presently sitting in were on fire, that would be a clear and present danger. You would seek a remedy. **LEAVE THE BUILDING!** Thus, a change has occurred. You took action.

On the other hand, if your boss presents you with a challenging new position with substantial rewards—e.g., financial, influence, power, etc.—you might view it as an opportunity. On a corporate level, if your company could meet an otherwise unmet customer need, this could have great advantage and serve as an opportunity. In either case, these events involve change.

The caveat of change comes with our individual desire or capability to deal with the opportunities and challenges. Our capacity as individuals and organizations to confront, respond to, and embrace change takes many forms. In a later chapter, we will discuss ways to build the ability to "spring back" when change occurs. But for now, let's look at the process of change.

Joe, John, and the ability and willingness to change

Our capability to adjust to, respond to, and even thrive in change is dependent upon many factors. These include our understanding of the change, what is involved in making the change, its impact upon us as individuals, the rewards for supporting or embracing the change, and the consequences of not supporting the change. Basically, our capacity for change involves our ability to change and our willingness to change.

Frequently we have the ability to do something, yet do not have the willingness. This is also true in reverse.

Notice what happens each morning when your alarm clock goes off. You have the ability to "rise and shine." Do you have the willingness? Is it difficult for you to change positions, to leave the comfort of your bed? Do you see the opportunities that await you at work that day? Do you see the danger of staying in bed—not going to work?

Several years ago, a friend and colleague of mine, named Joe, convinced me to learn to snowboard. Joe is several years younger than I. He is also in much better physical condition. And Joe had a strong desire to snowboard. (I also think he had a strong desire to watch me attempt to learn.) Well, after succumbing to Joe's incredibly persuasive personality, we planned our trip. Joe did the research to find a nearby ski slope that taught snowboarding. We took a day off from work. We got an early start so we could drive three hours to get to the slope.

By the time we arrived we were excited, yet anxious. We knew the dangers. We knew the risk of injury was fairly high. We knew that many of our colleagues at work were anxious to hear about our adventure and to see if we came back with broken bones.

We arrived at the ski slope dressed and ready for the day. We were both ready to learn and enjoy the adventure. It was a beautiful day. The sky was clear. It was cold enough to keep the snow frozen, yet warm enough to make it a pleasurable experience.

Joe and I paid for the lift tickets, then ventured to the rental shop to secure our snowboards. This is the point where the reality set in and the danger buzzer started to sound.

While I had seen snowboards before, I had never actually paid much attention to them and certainly never put one on my feet. Was I in for a surprise!

Unlike downhill or water skis, you get strapped to the board. I felt like I was being married to the board for the day. What would I do if I fell (which I was certain to do)? How would I get to the ski slope then put this *THING* on? Besides the practical considerations, there was the matter of form. You stand on the board sideways—not a natural position.

Next, we went to the ski school to arrange for lessons. As uneventful as that was, it allowed us enough time to question what we had decided to do, as well as question our sanity. At this point, our willingness to confront the challenge—the change—was disappearing. We began to realize that our ability to snowboard was very low. Then we had doubts about our ability to learn. It got to the point that we began questioning our willingness to even try.

The big moment arrived. We met the young, hot dog, winter-tanned instructor at the ski school slope. In case you're not familiar with skiing, the beginners' area is called the "bunny" hill, and it's generally used by children who are barely able to stand up, much less ski. Our pride was crushed. As we attempted to put on our boards and stand, we immediately understood why he asked us to go to this slope. Our desire to meet the challenge was melting fast.

As the day (actually it was only an hour) progressed, our willingness diminished. We seriously questioned our coach and ourselves. However, slowly, with clear guidance and mutual support, we gained skill and confidence. Suddenly, as quickly as it left us, our ability increased. As our ability increased, so did our willingness. By the end of the hour we were able to ride a chair lift and snowboard (falling regularly, however) down the slope.

So you see, life presents many challenges, self-induced and not. Do you see challenges as opportunities or dangers? We had to gain ability and regain our willingness to overcome the danger of our tackling our personal Mt. Everest and look for the opportunities. It wasn't easy or obvious at first, but we did it. We found the opportunities for fun, fellowship, exercise, and the beauty of our surroundings and we learned how to snowboard.

Climbing your personal Mt. Everest

Joe and I tackled snowboarding because we wanted to do so. But what about the changes you face? They aren't always by choice and they aren't always fun and rewarding.

Today, change is being caused by elemental shifts in the way we do our business and live our lives. For example, your grandfather probably held one job in his lifetime. Your father may have changed jobs every ten years, or two or three times in his career. If the averages hold true, you will probably change jobs at least every five years or more, given the speed and depth of change in work and how forces outside our control affect it.

A Sunday issue of the *New York Times* contains more information on one day than the average person was exposed to in his/her entire life just 100 years ago. In 1998, as many as 8,000 Americans joined the "home-working" environment each day. Many of the changes that occur are so complex and uncharted that we need new knowledge, new training, new vocabularies just to do the work we've always done.

Change keeps on coming, whether we're ready, willing, and able or not. So, how do we tackle the climb or "challenges" that come our way? Step by step.

Endings and Beginnings

With every change there is an ending and a beginning. The ending occurs when we decide for ourselves that the old way of doing things will stop and we will embrace the new. This changeover can happen in a few moments or it may take several years to occur. Endings and beginnings take on many forms, such as:

- Death
- Firing
- Reassignment
- Divorce
- Company purchased
- Graduation
- Person no longer present
- Unemployment/new employment
- New job/responsibilities
- Aloneness
- New ownership
- Entering the "work world"
- New product line

The period of transition between the ending and the new beginning is a critical stage. It is during this time that we face a high degree of uncertainty, instability, confusion, and emotional stress.

At this point of transition many questions arise. We wonder what was wrong with the way things were? We may ask who decided to make this change. Other frequently asked questions include: What's going to happen to me? Will I lose my job? Will my pay be affected? Will I need to learn new skills? When will the other shoe drop?

What's in it for me?

Keep in mind that we are all tuned in to the same radio station in our minds. We all listen to station WII-FM: "What's In It-For Me." This is our frame of reference, our starting point. This is the point from which we view the world, events, the lives of others, and, most significantly, our own lives. We start here. "What's in it for me?" It's not selfish. It's not irresponsible. It's just the way it is.

When we encounter change, it is helpful to understand that our "self" reactions, our need for self-preservation, are normal. We all have the same thought, whether we admit it or not. Maybe we respond differently. Maybe we react differently. But the bottom line is the same. We all have the same point of reference, "What's in it for me?" And that's okay.

There's no need to feel guilty, or egotistical, or self-centered because you are looking out for your own best interest. There's nothing wrong with liking things the way they are if they are right for you. It's natural to want to feel comfortable in your surroundings. It's also natural to feel a little negative about change, because change often challenges your personal expectations and world views.

Accept your feelings of self-preservation as natural. It'll make your transition from endings to new beginnings less trying.

TYPES OF CHANGE

We know that change is a regular occurrence. We know that it is likely to continue to recur. We know that we all question the "what's in it for me" aspect. So, let's consider three types of changes we encounter in our day-to-day and corporate lives: minor, significant, and traumatic.

Minor Change

We might call minor change the inconvenience we experience on a regular basis. In fact, minor change is so commonplace that we learn to adapt and adjust to it without much of a second thought. The amount of disruption that occurs with this type of change is minimal and generally inconsequential.

Most people who live in major metropolitan areas and commute to work, for example, develop alternate routes. This allows them to adjust their path to produce the least impact. In other words, they adjust, or change, their routine in order to deal with the minor changes resulting from accidents, tie-ups, construction, and the like.

Or consider flying. Aircraft are off course about 90 percent of the time. While pilots have a clear focus or direction, the paths of other air traffic, turbulence, and air traffic controller instructions contribute to the need for adjustment. Fortunately, navigational and guidance systems are constantly at work making the necessary adjustments to lead the aircraft and its passengers to the correct destination. If these adjustments were not in place, instead of leaving New York and landing in Charlotte, North Carolina, you might end up in Atlanta.

Significant Change

The second type of change is of a more significant nature. It may happen to individuals and organizations every two years or so. This is the type of change that involves a substantial shift in expectations because the course of our lives and our organizations are significantly impacted.

Examples might include a new job assignment that we were not expecting, or the sudden opportunity to expand into a new market. In these cases we are able to adjust, but it takes a concerted, deliberate effort and commitment of resources.

Traumatic Change

Trauma is the third, and most serious, type of change. It occurs on relatively rare occasions and involves a major adjustment in expectations and a significant expenditure of resources. Examples of traumatic change in our personal life would include marriage, divorce, a first born child, starting a new career, or the death of a loved one.

In organizations, traumatic change might involve a merger, acquisition, downsizing, new technology, or new operating procedures. Traumatic change is not the type of change that we experience often enough, so we are usually less likely to be prepared for the demands that come with it.

✳ ✳ ✳

"So Maggie, we can't avoid change but we can make it more palatable by knowing what change is and understanding how it affects us. Minor changes or inconveniences practically take care of themselves with little or no effort. Significant changes take work and resources but they can be surmounted," I reiterated. "But it's the traumatic changes like you and your coworkers keep facing that take strength, determination, and resources. You can and will make it through traumatic changes. People do it every day."

"I guess if I have the option of looking at change as an opportunity or danger, I'd much rather choose opportunity," Maggie said with a smile. "And there will be a clean slate to start with after the change is made. I guess I'm stuck in the middle right now...in between old and new because I'm wondering if this change makes any sense. But if that's normal...I'm okay with it. When I really stop and think about it, there are certainly a lot of new possibilities in it for me. You know, this could work out fine..."

2 | Our Responses to Change

"The only person who likes change is a wet baby."
—Price Pritchett

Christmas time at Granny's was a real treat. No matter how old we were, no matter that we kids had our own kids, nieces, and nephews, we could always count on a magical Christmas holiday at Granny's place. That was one thing Granny would never change. I think it would definitely signal danger rather than opportunity if anything changed!

Christmas also brought the neighbors together, so I wasn't too surprised to see Maggie dipping into the eggnog the December following our first meeting.

"So Maggie, how's everything going?" "Just so, John," she said rather perplexed. "You know, I thought I understood change...and yes, I could see the things you described happening, but it's been six months now. My office mate is driving me nuts. I can't take her negativity any more. I want to shake her and tell her to get over it...but she's constantly bad-mouthing management, being sarcastic and always depressed... she makes me so angry...and then they put me in charge of this 'change' team...Team? We can't agree on anything. Bob refuses to budge. He's been there forever and likes it the way it was. David, on the other hand, always has these off-the-wall ideas and he's off on a tangent out there somewhere. We can't reel him in. We're getting nowhere..." Maggie stopped and looked at me. "I'm sorry John, it's Christmas..."

"Hey, Mag, I understand. Maybe it's time to learn some more about change. Not everybody responds to change the same way, you know. We've all got our own time lines, our own little quirks, our own styles of coping with change."

"I know that...I think..." she said. "Ugh...I don't know what I know anymore. Wow, you think you've got all the answers after you get that MBA. But, at least there's one thing I do know for sure," she raised a cup of punch to toast me, "I do know it's Christmas, so cheers!"

Change prompts many responses. Some are physical; some are emotional; some psychological; others, intellectual. Sometimes in the midst of change, we suddenly find it hard to concentrate and focus our attention. We lose trust in ourselves. We lose trust in others and teamwork can be hampered. We may lose sleep, or maybe the number of errors we make increases. Why? Because the way we trust the world to operate becomes disoriented.

Once people have created a particular way of understanding the world, they tend to hold on to it quite strongly. That's why it is so hard to change anything of substance in organizations—i.e., shared philosophies, values, assumptions, beliefs, expectations, norms, etc.

According to Kilman, et al, there are three reasons for this. First, people typically form routine practices, assumptions, and values over a long period of time that smooth the way for productivity and workable relationships. Thus their conclusions feel like reality. This points us in a mode or focus that, from our point of view, requires no challenge. Our way is **THE** accepted way. A second reason is, simply, people often do not want their culture to change. Finally, some people are able to enforce a particular view of the world, values, and practices because their organizational position, control, or resources allows them the power to do so.

Parker J. Palmer wrote, "We want a kind of knowledge that eliminates mystery and puts us in charge of an object-world. Above all, we want to avoid a knowledge that calls for our own conversion. We want to know in ways that allow us to convert the world— but we do not want to be known in ways that require us to change as well."

In other words, we want others to see things as we see them, and do things as we do them. Others can change their ways to accommodate ours. We don't want to change. We're comfortable as we are.

Change is something we love and hate; yet change is action, movement, life, and we know that without it our organizations, relationships, and our selves would die.

Phases of Change

Let's consider how we respond to this ever-changing world.

Because the speed, complexity, and volume of change are increasing, it is necessary that we develop more effective ways of coping with change. Our approaches to change must evolve or we will be left behind in the dust. When we are informed or become aware of changes, proposed or imposed, we generally start at a point of being uninformed and somewhat skeptical. This may be referred to as the state of unconscious incompetence. We do not know what we do not know, and that is all right.

As we gain more information, knowledge about the change and how it impacts us personally and professionally, we tend to resist and find ways to deface the situation. Our level of doubt about the change is high. We generally do not believe the change is appropriate, much less necessary, and we may question the ability—our own or that of our leaders—to effectively implement it.

At this point we make a decision to "buy in" to the program, or "check out" of it. People who "check out" are those who quit their jobs mentally but stay physically. We will consider those who choose to "buy into" the changes, versus those who do not and either stay or leave.

Informed Optimism

The next phase of response is when we gain more information and knowledge about the change and its impact. As our understanding and acceptance increases we approach a point at which we are informed and become optimistic. In other words, we move from being uninformed and skeptical to being informed and realistic. This we'll call the stage of conscious incompetence: We know what we don't know.

At this point, as our level of knowledge increases, the level of commitment to the change should increase. It's at this juncture that we reach a point of informed optimism and the stage of conscious competence: We know what we know.

This is where we accept the change and realize that we can make it work and that the positive aspects of the change offset the negative impacts.

Finally, when the change is completed, we gain a sense of satisfaction knowing that the change is complete and completed well.

Resistance to Change

If change is evident and change is constant, why don't we all just accept change and move on? It is because the everyday world is made up of individual realities. Here are a few of the most frequently cited reasons for resisting change:

- Loss of control
- Loss of money
- Loss of position/status
- Lack of preparation
- Comfort of a routine

- Ignorance about the reasons for change
- Personalizing the change
- Fear of the unfamiliar
- Pain from past experiences with change
- Lack of trust in leaders
- Lack of clear understanding
- Fear of the unknown
- Fear of the known
- Not wanting to be the first to enthusiastically agree
- Status quo
- Too much change already; when will this stop?

When old ways die

It is normal to grieve the loss of "the way it used to be" when we're in transition from an ending to a new beginning. Elisabeth Kubler-Ross, noted authority on the human response to death and dying, defines five distinct stages of the death/dying response (for those are dying as well as those who are grieving). Keep in mind that although these stages are presented in sequential order, not every person will go through the stages in the same order, or at the same time, nor will all people necessarily go through all the stages. Some people may even get stuck in certain stages and never go beyond.

THE GRIEVING PROCESS
Denial

The first stage is denial, which often functions to cushion the impact of the change. At this point we may say, "This will go away," "This too shall pass," "We've seen these ideas come and go so quickly, this one will be forgotten by our leaders in a few months, if not weeks."

Many years ago I was a senior leader in an organization that announced one of the largest, most far-reaching, complex, and expensive changes ever announced by the corporation. At the time, many of my colleagues and employees throughout the organization responded with statements like "Yeah, sure. I'll believe it when I see it," "We'll never see this happen," "We have never done anything this big before, it will be like all the announced changes, it will be off the 'radar screen' in a few months when the next big change will be announced," and on and on. If we don't acknowledge it, maybe it will go away.

Anger

Next is anger. At this point we get upset about the change because suddenly we realize it may have a negative impact on us, our families, and our co-workers. We may lash out with responses that include statements that are later regretted and acts that border on (if not cross the line into) insubordination.

Bargaining

At the stage of bargaining we think the change project can be altered. "We are different." "The severance package needs to be modified because I am unique." "The plan needs to be delayed so I can finish another project." "The way we do things at this location is different, so the changes will need to be modified to meet our unique way of doing things. The procedures we use works well for us. Even though the plan is to standardize, we will need a variance."

Depression

Next is the stage that I sometimes refer to as the stage of "organizational meltdown" or "a prozac moment," the stage of depression. It's that period when we begin to doubt ourselves, our friends, or our colleagues and question the idea of change. "Can we survive the stress of the change and can the organization endure the pressures of change?" This is also the point when acceptance of the change may begin, because we finally admit that it's a done deal.

Acceptance

Finally, we fully accept the change. We realize we can make it or have made it through the change. We can survive and possibly even thrive in the world of change. We can see the positive results of the working through the negative impacts of the change efforts. We may find ourselves saying, "These owners aren't so bad," or "Well, now I have a new career," or even "I guess these new skills I have to learn will make me more marketable." The key is that we accept the change and are ready to move on.

Reaching the point of acceptance enables individuals and organizations to more effectively implement the change. It's important to remember, however, that it takes much longer for some people to adapt to change than others. Since each person's response to the change may vary, the speed and ease with which they process the change will also vary. Much of this response will be based on past experience with change, the personal and professional impacts of the change, and individual change styles.

Different strokes for different folks

Futurist Joel Barker has written that doing things new ways puts everyone practicing the old ways at risk. The higher one's position the greater the risk. Thus the better you are at your position, the more you have invested in it, the more you have to lose when you change.

Recently I had a client that was undertaking a number of very large, complex, and critical changes. As I worked with several employee groups throughout the organization at various sites throughout the nation, I began to discover a difference in how people prepare for change.

When I asked people to identify when the last major or traumatic change had occurred in the organization, most of the groups identified events during the past three to five years. One group, however, surprised me. They were from a different part of the organization. They agreed that the last major change that had occurred happened more than ten years earlier. I was shocked. As I continued to work with this group I discovered a significant difference in their ability to cope with the changes.

The groups that had experienced change more recently were better able to see these changes in the context of a continuum and appeared better prepared for the personal and professional adjustments necessary, including relocation or outside employment. The group that had not experienced recent change, however, appeared to lack basic change-related coping skills, lacked confidence in the organization, and in themselves.

When life skips a beat

When I think of the effect that traumatic events have our lives, the vivid image that often comes to mind relates to an "old" record player.

You may recall phonographs. They were popular before compact disks and digital recordings. On occasion, when a record album was playing, the table might get jarred and the needle would be jarred causing it to move across the record. For a moment you weren't sure if it had skipped off the song or if it had been moved forward or backward. You were confused. The same is true when we experience traumatic change. We are shuffled. We may be lost. We experience confusion. We need time to adjust. We need information to assess where we are, where we are going, and to make a plan.

✳ ✳ ✳

"All right John, let me get this straight. Even if we all face the same change, we will all handle the change differently. When we change we feel confusion, we feel loss. We're giving up old, comfortable ideas and situations, so we go through a grieving process. To add to the confusion, we all grieve at our own pace in our own way. At least some of us do...some of us get stuck and never make it through...then we just kind of plod along not caring one way or the other," Maggie said as she looked up from her notepad. "O.K. that kind of explains why I'm confused and why my office mate is behaving the way she is. I guess I'll just have to accept it and hope she'll get over it.

Maybe I can help her somehow...but what about my 'change' team, I'm totally out of control on that one" Maggie continued, "We've got such different ideas and ways of doing things, I could scream."

"Have you ever considered using those differences to your advantage?" I asked Maggie.

"No. I never even thought about it. How would I know these things, John? Hey, is this what you call conscious incompetence?"

"You are a good student, Maggie," I said "Now about those differences. You said Bob is stuck in the past, David is somewhere in the future and you're in the middle kind of trying to pull it all together, is that correct?"

"Yes."

"What kind of guys are Bob and David?"

"Bob? He's a numbers guy. He's extremely methodical. No gray areas for him. David is kind of artsy, flighty, intelligent, and very creative."

"And you? I'm the practical one I guess. I see both sides. We need to keep some of the old ways that work, but find new ways to improve operations. With all the new technology, that shouldn't be hard."

"Excellent, then according to the Change Style Indicator, you have a well-balanced balanced team. You have someone who can provide creative ideas, someone who can provide practical solutions and someone to follow up."

"The 'Change Style' what?"

✳ ✳ ✳

Frequently in workshops and seminars I use the "Change Style Indicator" (CSI), developed by Drs. W. Musselwhite and Robyn D. Ingram of The Center for Creative Leadership. According to Musselwhite and Ingram, change style is, in part, a reflection of personality style. The CSI is an assessment tool they designed to measure preferred style in approaching change and dealing with situations involving change.

In this assessment, participants self-score an instrument which places them on a change style continuum ranging from Conserver to Pragmatist to Originator. Each style exhibits distinct differences and preferences when approaching change.

Understanding the dynamics involved in change styles can help those people who are initiating change better understand the reason for many common roadblocks to effective change including why some people are so threatened by change that they sabotage it; why some people are willing to take big risks and others can't handle even the smallest calculated risks; why some people get stuck and are unable to adapt to a change situation; why some people can see both the advantages and disadvantages of an issue while others cannot.

The three change style personalities are: Conservers, who prefer to preserve the existing structure and favor gradual and continuous improvement while using existing resources; Originators, who prefer fast, radical change which challenges existing structures; and Pragmatists, who prefer functional changes which take individual situations into account. The following is a brief summary of the three styles and their preferences for approaching change.

Conserver

- Accepts the paradigm
- Prefers change that is incremental
- Focuses on relationships
- Provides a safe base for riskier operations
- Focuses on refinement and follow–through

Pragmatist

- Explores the paradigm
- Prefers change that is functional
- Focuses on shared objectives
- Provides a situational perspective
- Focuses on concrete aspects and implementation

Originator

- Challenges the paradigm
- Prefers change that is expansive
- Focuses on task
- Provides dynamics to bring about radical change
- Focuses on conceptualization and initiation

While the CSI does not measure the effectiveness of a change style, it can be a useful tool to help leaders understand different personality types found within organizations. It has proven to be very useful in the formation of effective teams.

In an ideal team situation it is most practical to have creative ideas, practical solutions, and follow-up, which means a blend of Conservers, Originators, and Pragmatists, if possible.

Conservers

Conservers are people who tend to get things done on schedule, work well within structured environments, attend to details, and get the facts. They are excellent on follow-through, which is vital to the success of any team effort, and they tend to provide stability by adhering to routines and rules. They are very efficient.

As their name implies, Conservers are conservative leaders who promote traditional values, expect the rules to be followed, reward those who follow rules and can be relied upon for being consistent and stable. Conservers, on the other hand, prefer a secure work environment, steady and consistent pace, and time and space to contemplate.

Their rigidness, however, may be an obstacle to innovation because they don't want to break the rules and they may be unyielding and set in their ways. Conservers are often perfectionists, which may hinder completion of tasks. They get stuck on small details and inconsistencies and, given enough time, Conservers can think things to extinction!

Originators

At the other side of the continuum we have Originators, or the idea people. They have a strong understanding of complex problems and serve as catalysts for change. They are strong conceptualizers, the visionaries, and they enjoy taking risks.

They prefer working independently, unrestrained by rules, and like to work on several projects at one time. Originators are intellectually challenging and they thrive on change. As leaders, Originators are energetic, enthusiastic, and constantly reorganizing. They like to develop their own leadership style and love to be in on the start-up phase.

Although Originators are catalysts for systematic change and are highly flexible, their failure to focus on the reality of the situation can be detrimental. They may overextend themselves and may appear stubborn. They usually won't adapt well to policies and procedures and they may overlook details and other people while concentrating on the big picture.

Pragmatists

In the middle, we have what Musselwhite and Ingram call Pragmatists. These are the people who address the needs of the organization as they arise. They get people to work together for the common interest and encourage cooperation and compromise to get problems solved. Pragmatists are organized for action, can see both the short- and long-range picture, and are practical. They get things done in spite of the rules, not because of them.

Pragmatists are flexible and adaptive to their environment; they enjoy harmony and hands-on experience. They are productive people who enjoy participatory events. Pragmatists are excellent at using past experiences to solve current problems, facilitating problem solving among people, building cooperation, and encouraging congruence between values and actions.

Unfortunately, for all their virtues, Pragmatists may be indecisive, may not promote ideas enough to bring them to fruition, and may try to please too many people at the same time. They can also appear to be unable to make a commitment and appear to be easily swayed.

Overall, approximately 25 percent of the people tested are Conservers, 25 percent are Originators, with 50 percent of the respondents falling in the middle of the continuum as Pragmatists.

✳ ✳ ✳

"OK," said Maggie. "This all makes sense. But how does this apply to my team?"

"You said David is creative and filled with ideas, right Maggie? I'd say that makes him an Originator. Bob is rigid and traditional, so he's probably a Conserver. What you have here is a pendulum swinging back and forth...eating precious time as it moves back and forth. Who does David take his ideas to?"

"Bob. Then Bob tells him it'll never work and that it's never been done...so David gets angry, goes off and thinks of more ideas. So..." Maggie stopped.

"Nothing ever actually gets started," I continued. "What your team needs is someone who recognizes these differences...someone who can work with them..."

"We need a pragmatist..." said Maggie, "someone who can kind of bring the two sides together."

"And who might that be?" I asked.

II

BUILDING THE CAPACITY TO SPRING BACK AND THRIVE

In Part II we examine resilience, the ability to spring back, and learn ways to build our capacity for resilience. What qualities make individuals and companies thrive and survive while others do not? We will also take a look at the five necessary traits of resilient people and organizations and find out how ordinary people can sharpen their abilities and incorporate these traits into their everyday lives to become extraordinary leaders.

3 | Resilience

"It is not the strongest of the species that will survive, nor the most intelligent, but the one most responsive to change."
—Charles Darwin

"Change is inevitable; growth is optional."
—John DeBerry, Grief Counselor, Chicago, IL

How is it that some people and some organizations respond well to change while others seem to struggle just to survive? What is it that makes the difference? I think I found that answer back when I was nine years old.

Some of the fondest childhood memories I have are of Granny. I remember those long summer visits with her. I remember her warmth, her hugs, the freedom she gave me to explore in the old barn at her home, the adventure of spending a week with Granny each summer. I remember sometimes just sitting and doing nothing with her. You may have similar fond memories.

Granny was born about 100 years ago, at the turn of the twentieth century. William McKinley was president of the United States, Queen Victoria was on the throne in England, and the United States was involved in the Spanish-American War. When Granny was born, no one had ever flown, had an X-ray, celebrated Mother's Day, received a blood transfusion, or owned a new Ford, Chrysler, or Chevrolet.

I remember Granny's cooking, the smell of hot yeast rolls coming out of the oven, her love, her affection, her advice, and her stories about the past. I remember sitting in her lap for hours looking at a scrapbook of photographs and clippings she had collected through the years. One of the photographs was of the flight of the Wright brothers, the very first flight. She lived near Kitty Hawk, North Carolina, where that historic flight took place, so it held very special meaning to her.

I especially remember our special "field trips," that she took me on each summer. Like the time we visited a natural history museum where a portion of a dinosaur and some bones were on display. I was amazed. The bones were huge. I couldn't even begin to imagine how big these creatures really were. I asked Granny if there were any more dinosaurs and she said no, they were extinct. Of course I asked why, and she proceeded to tell me the story about these huge, ponderous beasts that could run you down and eat you for a snack, while others were as quiet and docile as your favorite pet. "Boy, I'd sure like to be a dinosaur," I said. Then I thought about it for a minute..."If they were so big and strong, how come they didn't live?" "Because they didn't change, honey. They didn't adapt. They couldn't live in the changing environment. So they disappeared." "So if I was a dinosaur I wouldn't be here with you today, would I Granny?" "That's right," she said. "Then I never want to be a dinosaur," I said. Little did I know how true those words would be.

Of all the life lessons Granny taught me along the way, one of the most important was about adapting. Granny seemed to take everything in stride. She was extremely flexible. She adjusted and helped me adapt as we confronted the many changes life had in store. And this lesson has served me well.

✳ ✳ ✳

The changes we face today are unlike those faced by Granny or even by the dinosaur. Today, the speed, complexity, and volume of change is increasing at such a rate that we struggle to keep up. We need to discover, adapt, and practice new ways of coping with and leading change. The ways we have responded in the past may have worked, but, with the very nature of change changing we need new ways of coping. Our capacity for surviving and thriving through change must, and can, evolve.

Survival of the Resilient

One need not look far to see examples of individuals and organizations that have had to confront change. Business pages of the newspaper and news stories on television are filled with stories that reflect the dinosaurs and the grannies of the business world every day.

During the early 1900s, 85 percent of the country's workers were in agriculture. Now, agriculture involves less than three percent of the work force. The shift in labor was toward manufacturing, yet now, according to Price Pritchett in *The Employee Handbook of New Work Habits for a Radically Changing World*, during the decade of the 1980s, a total of 230 (46 percent) companies disappeared from the "Fortune 500" list—just like that!

In a *Houston Chronicle* article on December 3, 1998, the Chief Operating Officer of Mergerstat, a company that monitors mergers and acquisitions, was quoted as saying, "So far this year, 149 mergers worth $1 billion or more involving U.S. companies have been announced, for a total value of $886 billion. For all of 1997, by comparison, there were 110 such deals worth $359 billion." And, the America Online and Time Warner merger announced in 2000 totals more than $31 billion in annual revenue and affects more than 80 thousand employees.

What is it that separates the grannies from the dinosaurs? What is it that makes some people succeed in the face of adversity, while others give up? Why do some companies make it while others end up in the industrial wasteland?

Like the dinosaurs, companies that can't adapt to change become extinct, and it has become more and more apparent that to adapt successfully, one must be resilient. The key however, is that individuals within the company must also exhibit these traits of resiliency in order to help the company survive.

Today's dinosaurs

In this day and age of downsizing, re-engineering, and mergers, we are all potential dinosaurs. Take, for example, the ability to use computers. A friend of mine, in her late forties, was not fortunate enough to have developed computer skills in school, so when computers hit the business world she "had to get with the program or starve." Because she was flexible and open to change and education, she was able to make the transition, she was able to make the jump. She learned resilience from everyday life experiences, adapted to change, and moved on. Unfortunately many of her peers didn't see the need to "learn computers," and they are either unemployed or they are members of the "working dead," those people who show up and go through the motions because they're just biding their time.

What makes one person adapt to change, while others just sit back, become extinct, and potentially take the company along with them? It's a skill called resiliency or the ability to surmount the obstacles of trauma and thrive.

Resiliency isn't a new idea. It comes from the Latin root *re-salire*, which means to jump back. In the past, human behavior scientists looked at resiliency as invulnerability or harmless resistance to stress; however, they are now beginning to recognize resiliency in terms of coping capacities that are influenced by a variety of factors.

According to researchers, there are several skills necessary for individuals to be resilient. One of the strongest skills that show up at the top of most studies is the ability to be and feel connected to others. This is rather surprising for a culture that prides itself on its rugged individualism. People find strength and importance through others—ministers, mentors—outside their families. Resilient people also tend to have problem-solving skills; intelligence; an inquisitive mind; and a "learn and cope" attitude toward problems rather than a "victim and blame" attitude.

Although our personality or behavior has a strong bearing on our style of handling change, psychologists are now recognizing that adapting to change, or resiliency, is also a matter of attitude, or how we look at the problem, and how we view ourselves. In other words, people are most successful at changing when they believe in their ability to change. Researchers are also finding that individuals can learn new behaviors to help make them more resilient.

In the face of change, here are several skills you might want to hone or call upon to help you through the transition. The first is your insight. Use your perception to question things. Ask yourself profound questions and give honest answers. "What effect will this change really have on me personally and can I really handle it?" "Am I afraid of the change or am I afraid I cannot handle the responsibilities?" "If I am forced to assume other responsibilities am I really too busy, or am I too lax?"

Second, build relationships with people who can help you learn the things you need to know to make your transition smoother. Find people who are embracing the change and associate with them. Choose people who are positive influences, people who will elevate you, not bring you down.

Take the initiative...or the bull by the horns, so to speak. Take charge of your situation rather than letting it take charge of you. Decide what you can and cannot accomplish rather than be told. Decide what training you will need and ask for it. Offer solutions to problems you might come across. Use your creativity and rediscover your sense of humor. You'll find that change isn't the enemy you envisioned.

Long thought to be a result of personality, environment, and just plain luck, researchers are now acknowledging that resiliency skills can be "fostered" and "nurtured." To do this we have to get rid of preconceived notions of how to approach life and redefine goals, says Glenn Richardson of the University of Utah. "Tapping into resiliency is more spiritual. It means going back to your childlike nature: your curiosity and questioning nature, your playfulness, the innate morality and nobility that children have."

You are probably much more resilient than you think. Take a close look at yourself and a major change you've encountered in your lifetime. Examine how you handled this change successfully by answering the following questions:

- *What was the change?*
- *How did you feel in the beginning?*
- *Were the changes considered opportunities or were they thought of as dangers?*
- *How did you overcome the adversity of change?*
- *How did you feel in the end?*
- *If you hadn't made the change would you be where you are today?*

Now examine the change you are going through in your work environment today. How do you feel? What are the opportunities? How can you adjust your attitude to accept the change? How can you use your resiliency skills (humor, creativity, initiative, etc.) to adapt? If you don't make this change, where might you be tomorrow?

✳ ✳ ✳

Granny had the right idea. We may be able to run, but we cannot hide from change. If we are flexible, able to bend, we will make it through the change and become stronger. We can increase our adaptability by increasing our capacity for change. We can increase our capacity for change by adjusting our attitude as well as our behavior. We can take charge of change and use it to our advantage or we can fight it. We can adapt our behavior and attitudes. We can be survivors or we can be dinosaurs. It's our call.

4 | Survival of the Fittest

"The better adapted you are, the less adaptable you tend to be."
—**Gerald M. Weinberg, author, *The Secrets of Consulting***

"Hey Maggie, how's it going?" I said when I recognized the familiar voice on the phone. "I heard you've been promoted to manager, congratulations."

"Thanks, John. Those tips you gave me worked. When the change team finally got working together, we were dynamite. As for your question, things are going..." She sounded a bit distressed. "Production is down. Sales are down. So all of a sudden we're introducing a new line. We're getting a new computer system in manufacturing and it will mean all kinds of internal and external changes in equipment, personnel, operating procedures and then there's our new satellite links. As if things aren't chaotic enough, I have to train my new assistant who they finally approved after three months, and we are also in the process of..."

"Slow down, Maggie."

"John, I wouldn't feel so frazzled, but it seems like this happens every time. When sales drop, the top office gets all these ideas, they want to do them all! They just jump from idea to implementation. It's like they forget it takes some thought in between. And of course they expect their ideas to come to fruition and be successful... yesterday."

"Look Maggie, I know it doesn't make it any easier, but you'd be amazed how many companies do the same thing every day. They leap before they look. They skip the opportunity to take advantage of creative ideas that may have provided them with stronger end results. Instead they rush headlong and before you know it, they're back to square one and starting change all over again, and the next crisis, until one day they're out of business, wondering what happened."

"That's what has me frightened this time, John. What if we can't make it through these next changes?"

"Got a pencil, Maggie? O.K. Write this word down. Focus. Let's start with focus. Obviously, if this has happened so many times before, it's time for someone to step in and show some leadership skills. Are you game?"

"Me? I...I," Maggie stuttered then paused as if to think about it. "Why not? So what was that word? Focus. Lead on!"

✳ ✳ ✳

By studying individuals and organizations that have faced the challenges of change, one can see a pattern of characteristics that prevail.

According to Darryl L. Conner, author of *Managing at the Speed of Change: How Resilient Managers Succeed and Prosper Where Others Fail*, these are called the characteristics of resilience. These are simple yet critical tools, that, when applied, can engage a person or organization to survive and even thrive during the turbulence of change. The five characteristics are the ability to focus, to be proactive, to be positive, to be organized, and to be flexible.

ABILITY TO FOCUS

Organizations that survive and thrive know where they are going. They have a mission, a direction, a goal. They are focused.

In his book, *From Worst to First: Behind the Scenes of Continental's Remarkable Comeback*, Gordon Bethune writes of his experiences as CEO of Continental Airlines. He tells of spending an extraordinary amount of time and taking great pains to define a direction for the turnaround. While the issues he faced were complex and interrelated, Bethune led the way with the development of what he calls "a flight plan."

His plan was to take an airline, which was running at a loss of nearly $55 million per month, on the verge of bankruptcy for the third time in 10 years, and make it one of the best airlines in the nation.

According to Bethune, a leader is "the person who looks at the big picture and says, 'Okay, everybody, go west!'" Bethune is focused.

Martin Luther King, Jr., didn't lead a change in civil rights based on a statements like "I have some followers" or "I have some ideas." King clearly stated, "I have a dream." He was able to explain that dream in a way that you and I can understand. He was able to explain it in ways that his followers could embrace. And, most important, he was able to explain it in ways that set people toward the same goal: change. King was focused.

In the mid-1990s Stephen Covey and his team popularized the idea of establishing mission statements for organizations and individuals. Mission statements help focus the goals of a company toward a specific end and serve as a foundation for decision making and action during challenging times. Working with the end in mind, we have focus.

The Bible gives us several examples of direction and focus. In the Old Testament we can see the various directives from God including the Ten Commandments. Another example, this one from the New Testament, comes in the form of "The Great Commission": "Therefore go and make disciples of all nations..." (Matthew 28:19).

Focus on the finish and beyond

Former Herman Miller Chairman Max DePree tells the story of the person who was described as being good at running the 95-yard dash. He points out that running only 95 yards of a 100-yard dash makes the last five yards pointless. DePree completes the story by telling that a colleague explained that serious runners think of the 100-yard dash as a 110-yard dash so that no one will beat them in the last few yards. We all anticipate reaching the ribbon at the end of the 100-yard dash, but unless we strive and reach for 110, we may run out of steam and fall short.

Sharpen your focus

Through workshops and seminars I have asked participants to share their ideas for improving resilience. Here is a list of some of the valuable ideas they have shared for becoming more focused. I hope they will work for you, and I hope you'll add your own.

To establish and act on priorities, I can:

- Select several goals and follow a plan to realize them without having so many goals that I don't achieve any
- Stay in touch with the "big picture" in my department
- Remember this training period won't last forever; concentrate and get it done right the first time
- Decrease the amount of time in non-urgent, non-important activities
- Determine a clear vision of what needs to be accomplished
- Center on the task at hand, don't get wrapped up in the unknowns or past mistakes
- Concentrate on a single topic at a time and follow through
- Create a list of action items that are needed to keep me positive about the changes

In addition to organization goals, workshop participants thought personal goals were important to have to see them through change. Here are some of their thoughts:

- Continue to pray on a daily basis
- Do one thing at a time, don't start a lot of small projects
- Exercise to increase my stamina
- Stick to my goals and guidelines
- Look to the future and envision my objectives, then start to take the steps to reach them
- Write more specific, smaller goals to enable me to be more focused on the goals that need to be accomplished
- Make becoming computer literate a priority

BECOME PROACTIVE

Sometimes people wait for things to happen. These are people I call "effect people." They are the ones that "things" always seem to happen to. The car breaks down every week, the kids are sick, the competitor won the contract. You know the type. They always wonder what happened and why things always happen to them?

Then, there are those people and organizations that make things happen. They take the lead. They are on the edge. They create winning situations. They are proactive. They don't wait for events and circumstances to occur; they create them. I call this "creating the future" or "making things happen."

Another way to look at this is to consider that organizations have preventive maintenance and process improvement programs designed to create quality. They have strategic planning processes and systems to look into the future and set directions. How many actually follow those principles? How many individuals create contingencies and ways of preparing for the future?

I recently read that the average American waits until age 29 to begin saving for retirement, yet hopes to retire before age 60. It is estimated that most will not, however, have the resources to retire with adequate income until after the age of 65. Consider the positive impact of more proactive behavior in this situation: start saving a few years earlier, sacrifice for the future, be patient, and know that your action is yielding good consequences.

Steps to make things happen

Here are some ideas from my workshop participants for improving capacity in the area of being more proactive. Try them on for size, take them for a test drive. Create your own approaches. Find someone who is particularly good in this area. Study that individual. Ask them to be your coach. Look for other organizations that seem to lead the edge. Take a cue from a famous sports shoe manufacturer and just do it!

I can do it if I...

- Bring my own ideas/suggestions to fruition alone or with other appropriate people (quit dreaming, start doing)
- Just get started to begin the process of doing the other four parts of being resilient
- Seek ways to accomplish goals rather than have them decided for me
- Develop a plan to act upon
- Plan ahead for change rather than defend against it
- Keep an open mind; don't make quick judgments
- Seek out and implement ways to overcome computer fear
- Develop a system to process rush orders and meet deadlines
- Make a weekly goals list to prepare for career changes
- Start learning skills that will help me get a job when my job is eliminated in a few months
- Prepare for a career change by taking at least one appropriate training course
- Become more proactive in my relationships with staff I supervise by encouraging dialog and coaching to prepare them for the changes
- Stay aware of my surroundings and one step ahead
- Look for change and prepare ahead of time
- Prepare for meetings and work sessions

BE POSITIVE

A third characteristic of resilient individuals and organizations is that they are positive. This does not mean denying the existence of problems or believing that problems will take care of themselves. They are not Pollyannas. It means living your life, doing your work, running your business and yes, facing challenges, with a sense of optimism.

Again, Max DePree gives us a valuable lesson when he says, "Giants see opportunities where others see trouble." Be positive.

Bobby's Biggest Challenge

Optimism brings to mind an outstanding athlete I attended high school with in the early 1970s. Bobby was a star on the baseball field and on the track. He was also a very good student with many academic achievements. He was certain to receive a full athletic scholarship to one of the big universities.

41

Unfortunately, on his way home from baseball practice one spring afternoon the motorcycle on which he was riding skidded on some loose gravel as he rounded a curve. He slid into an intersection and under the wheels of an oncoming delivery truck. His body was badly mangled. His right leg was damaged so severely that after several weeks and many attempts to save it, amputation was required. This, of course, forever shattered his hopes of college sports.

That fall, Bobby returned to school without the leg and with crutches. As he stumbled to class and worked to regain his strength you could see the pain and anger in his face. Here was the young man who had it all. Now, his dreams and hopes were gone.

By spring, doctors and therapists had taught him to walk with a prosthetic leg. Bobby continued to struggle to walk and regain his energy for life. One day as we walked down the hall to class I asked him how he was coping with the changes in his life. I told him that I was sure he was angry and frustrated. I assumed he felt his dreams and possibly his life were forever ruined. I asked about his anger over the artificial leg.

Bobby replied, "John, this leg does not have me. I have it! And, it always reminds me to do all that I can do and be all that I can." Now, that was a powerful lesson for me.

Stay positive

Here are a few suggestions from peers for ways to improve your sense of being positive during change. I can remain positive if I...

- Focus on how much opportunity I have ahead of me
- Keep a sense of humor
- Develop a better appreciation for the "little things" that make this a special place
- Increase communication with my boss (mentor type) for support
- Say one positive thing about the change each day
- Be more patient
- Focus on the good things, don't dwell on the negative
- Resolve to reduce the negative conversations about people at headquarters, avoid gossip
- Evaluate each day by what I accomplished rather than by what did not get done
- Work on maintaining and improving morale (my own and those with whom I work)
- Be thankful for what I have
- See success and learning experiences but avoid labeling things that didn't go as expected as "failures"
- Remind myself that "I can get through this"

- Remember to count to ten
- Think positively...act positively

GET ORGANIZED

To be able to respond to the turbulent winds of change we must be focused, proactive, and positive. When we know where we want to go, what we want to achieve, and the changes that must be made in our businesses and ourselves, we have to act on them. To do this requires a plan. To carry out a plan effectively, we have to be organized.

While this may seem obvious, why is it that we all have 24 hours a day, yet some of us have time to achieve everything we want while others don't even have time to get started? Time may be the great equalizer, but it's how you use time that counts. As Ben Franklin said, "To fail to plan is to plan to fail." Now is the time to dig out of the clutter, toss away the extraneous, and get organized.

Improve resilience through organization

There are hundreds of ways to clean out our minds and offices. The following list gives some of the favorites of managers who have participated in my workshops. They may be simple and common sense, but sometimes we need gentle reminders to reach us through the clutter! I can become organized if I...

- Keep a "to do" list and use it
- Put everything in its place consistently and check myself three times per week
- Put my office in order, files neat and efficient
- Attack procrastination
- Update my telephone directory
- Answer each day's mail as it comes in; throw away junk mail
- Actually use my Covey planner, not just carry it around
- Throw out stuff
- Learn to say no to people when asked to take on more than I know I can handle
- Follow through
- Start files for all the "stuff" on my desk
- List all my job functions as "do" and overdue, then prioritize them
- Organize my desk and file
- Use agendas for meetings I lead
- Look at the big picture and then take a section at a time
- Reduce the number of "low priority" projects and involvement
- Use travel and hotel time to do planning and correspondence

FLEXIBILITY

The final characteristic of resiliency is flexibility. Mistakes and course corrections are a natural side effect of change efforts. Sometimes this means the budget is inadequate or suppliers cannot deliver as expected. Perhaps the competition turns up the heat to increase pressure, or new solutions to problems are offered. Resilient individuals and organizations have their focus and their plan. They also have the ability to adjust to achieve their goals.

In late 1998, the B. F. Goodrich Company received criticism for moving from its home in Akron, Ohio to Charlotte, North Carolina. Statements in the press chastised company leaders for abandoning their heritage in the city known as the tire capital of the nation. What may have been lost is the fact that B. F. Goodrich had re-invented itself several years earlier. Tire manufacturing was no longer a part of its product mix. Goodrich became something else. It was adept at change and demonstrated agility to become a totally new company.

Increase flexibility

Here are some examples of ways to increase flexibility on a personal, professional and organizational level provided by managers who were experiencing change.

- Learn to go with the flow
- Get rid of "black/white" thinking
- Be more spontaneous
- Become more open to other people's suggestions and ideas
- Be willing to do things in new ways (without trying to make the new methods resemble the old)
- Remember a change is not always planned but you make the plan to accomplish that change
- Let people work on their own...let it go!
- Revise priorities as needed...and quickly
- As we go through changes at work and I am required to work longer hours, plan ahead at home by preparing meals, clothes, etc., to help make it less stressful and give me more freedom
- Be patient, listen, react softly
- Expect some things to go wrong and realize that it's okay
- Recognize that day-to-day priorities change and be more open to these changes
- Accept changes I cannot influence

* * *

"You know, John, I never thought about things like flexibility, or the differences in the way people respond to change. And that stuff about grieving..." Maggie paused to sip her cappuccino. "It's all starting to make sense when I look at everyone around me...and now that I have a better understanding of the work styles, or the CSI, of my co-workers, I think I can help them become more resilient...and help myself, too."

"How so?" I challenged my prized pupil.

"Well take Bob...as a Conserver. He's going to hold on for dear life. He doesn't like change, plain and simple. He's a nervous wreck, afraid to do anything that crosses the lines. But now that I understand that, I realize that that doesn't make him wrong or stubborn. Maybe I can help him become less rigid by empathizing, and showing him slowly that change isn't necessarily horrible or wrong. It's just going to take awhile and a lot of patience."

I knew she was onto something and wanted to encourage her train of thought. "That's true...now what about David, the flighty one?"

"Oh, I think I'll buy him some great new toys...I'll encourage the kid in him. He's a great role model for resiliency. When you think about it, he's like a giant bungee cord...he stretches and springs back constantly...Even when people think he's gone off the deep edge, he doesn't care. He keeps at it until they come around one way or the other. And even if they don't buy his ideas, he keeps giving us a fresh, new look at things."

"So flighty isn't so bad after all?" I questioned.

"Well, it has it's place. When you understand it...and you learn to use it, rather than let it use you," she smiled.

"And what about Maggie, can she adapt?" I wondered out loud.

"Yes, I think I can...actually I am adapting," said Maggie, "and I wasn't aware of it. I'm not fighting it any more or feeling as frustrated. When I thought about challenges I had in my past, like leaving home to go to college out of state, I realized that change wasn't so awful after all. I was terrified. I was afraid that I wouldn't know anybody and I didn't. But I looked at it from the perspective that most of the other students were in the same boat. And I made a conscious effort to be friendly. It didn't take long before I had loads of friends and I forgot about being afraid. I guess I had made it worse in my head, fear of the unknown you know..." she paused. "If I hadn't changed my life and gone away, I don't think I'd be where I am today. I know it's hindsight, but change wasn't so bad...I lived to talk about it. I adapted. And I realize that I've changed quite a bit since I've been talking with you. Understanding helps...being prepared for the ups and downs helps...learning about the way people respond and why they respond the way they do...it all helps..."

I said, "Becoming a little more flexible in your outlook are you?"

Maggie nodded her head in agreement. I knew we were definitely making progress.

Increase your capacity for change action plan

"John, everything you said about flexibility and resiliency is just common sense so why didn't I think of these things myself. They're so easy," said Maggie. "You know, I think I'll take the five ingredients for resiliency and present them to everyone at a company meeting. This way I can become more proactive. And maybe by sharing my knowledge with my co-workers I can maybe help them analyze their own perceptions of change."

"That's a great idea, Maggie. Sometimes common sense has to be brought out, encouraged through gentle reminder," I said. "Here's an action plan to help you increase your capacity for change. Develop a worksheet, such as the one on page 93, to help you organize your personal and team for action. I guarantee, it will help improve resilience all around."

✳ ✳ ✳

"Thanks John, this is great. Now see if I got it right. Your capacity for resilience can be increased by strengthening your abilities to focus, to be proactive, to be positive, to be organized, and to be flexible."

"Perfect Maggie. And you can start by focusing on being proactive. Now get to work on your action plan and start the wheels rolling."

"I know—today. Thanks John."

✳ ✳ ✳

Not too long after that, Maggie called to say that she had taken her action plan to her chief operating officer (COO). He was very impressed with her initiative and her ideas and agreed to her holding a meeting to share the five steps with the rest of the company. He also thanked her for giving him a wake-up call of sorts by starting the ball rolling. He didn't know where to start, and he admitted that needed a refresher course on resiliency himself.

He realized that it had been too long since he had really sat down and took an overall look at exactly what was going on in his small, but relatively profitable, company. He at least had the sense of humor to laugh when he realized that he was too busy to take care of everyday business ever since he got involved in making changes, but then he also realized that for his company to stay afloat in today's market, there'd be plenty more changes ahead. Maggie and her COO had a long talk about resiliency, and he thanked her for making him stop and think about what exactly it will take for the company to make it this time. He agreed that it was time to get organized, to focus on where the company was heading. He invited Maggie and a team that she would personally select, to develop a company mission statement as a starting point. He thanked Maggie for taking the initiative to come in and share her concerns and her ideas.

When she walked out of that office, she was energized and inspired. For the first time since she started working, Maggie actually felt like she had a promising future ahead of her at the company. Now, all she had to do was organize an effective team to work with. How difficult could that be?

✳ ✳ ✳

In a perfect meeting we'd all have the same opinions, the same agendas, the same feelings, the same way of processing information, and we'd be in perfect agreement and ready to leave in five minutes or less. Fortunately, we don't all act the same or think the same, even though that does make for some pretty long meetings.

Unfortunately, it's this variety in thought processes that can get us into trouble when we are trying to work as a team.

Maggie learned this lesson fast. It was the first time she ever had to work with engineers, technicians, plant workers, and the company's Chief Financial Officer (CFO). Her Originator teammate (remember the Change Style Indicator?), who was still in left field after all this time, would also be involved.

She had prepared a very clever, full-screen presentation for the first session. She knew everyone would enjoy it, be pumped up and ready to contribute.

Following the presentation, David gave her a thumbs up; the sales and marketing people started talking amongst themselves, furiously writing notes. Ed and Sam from the plant just kind of sat quietly looking around the room, while Steve, the chief engineer, and Randall, the CFO, sat looking at the blank screen with blank looks on their faces.

"So," Maggie said enthusiastically, "what does everyone think?" The room went silent and she felt this sudden helpless feeling as the silence grew louder.

✳ ✳ ✳

"What did I do wrong John? I gathered my team together based on their CSI scores and by all indicators they should have been incredibly responsive. I had the entire mix, the perfect blend of Originators, Conservers, and Pragmatists. At least I thought I did. And I got nothing, absolutely nothing. No response."

"Well Maggie, while the Change Style Indicator (CSI) reveals the style with which people react to change, there is another valuable a tool that can provide additional insight, actually get you into their brain. It's called the HBDI or Herrmann Brain Dominance Inventory."

THE HERRMANN BRAIN DOMINANCE INVENTORY

Created by the late Ned Herrmann while he was doing research related to thinking and to how the brain functioned, The Herrmann Brain Dominance Inventory (HBDI) goes beyond the more common models of left/right brain dominance that are quite familiar to most people.

Unlike left/right brain dominance tests that basically define personality (the Change Style Indicator), the HBDI is a self-administered inventory tool designed to look at thinking styles. This proves very valuable in achieving excellence in the areas of leadership, teamwork, and communication.

The model looks metaphorically into four quadrants, four thinking styles or four different thinking selves found within the brain. These selves include the rational self, the safe-keeping self, the feeling self, and the experimental self. (See Appendix B, "Whole Brain Model" on pages 94 and 95, and Appendix C, "Our Different Selves on pages 96 and 97.)

The premise of the HBDI model is that we all have thinking styles and our thinking style comes from what we're interested in. What we're interested in obviously has something to do with what our motivations are, therefore, what our competence is.

For example, people who are interested in numbers, finances, and other analytical kinds of thought and activities, are more likely to do things that fall into that category. They might be accountants, or scientists looking at research data. These "A" quadrant types would be considered rational or analyzers.

"B" quadrant or self-keepers are the action takers, the people who are good at getting things done and who are good at establishing and keeping policies. As a change leader, it is helpful to know that these are the last people to approach when a change must take place because chances are they are the people who created the policies that are going to be changed and they may initially be resistant.

The third area of brain dominance, or "C" quadrant, is the feeling self, the sensitive, talkative person who is concerned with human aspect of change. Teachers fall into this category.

Finally, we have the experimental self, or "D" quadrant, the people who speculate, take risks, who break the rules and push the envelope. These are the entrepreneurs, the designers. People who explore the options.

Keep in mind when you look at the four different selves that each of us has bits and pieces of each of these styles. We are not generally solely any one. As a matter of fact at least 60 percent of the population is dominant in at least two of the quadrants. However, only 30 percent is dominant in three and a mere 3.5 percent of the population is dominant in all four areas.

So how can this knowledge make you a more effective change leader? If you understand how and why you think the way you do, and how and why others think the way they do, you will be able to combine the best of all thought patterns to develop a "whole brain" approach to change.

What is your thinking style?

Before you continue, you may want to determine what your thinking style is. See Appendix B, "Whole Brain Model" on pages 94 and 95. The whole brain models and "different selves" quadrant diagrams will provide you with basic understanding of your style.

III

ORGANIZATIONAL COMPONENTS

Now we will explore the four critical components of successful change efforts. They are leadership, teamwork, project/action planning, and management and communication. Each is addressed in the context of change efforts and change-oriented environments.

You might view these key elements as the foundation blocks for building successful change. Why do I focus on these key components and not the myriad of important leadership and management skills, experiences, and abilities? These components were selected based on my personal experiences working as a consultant with major corporations.

Experience has shown that the absence of, or a weak presence of, these four basic elements, results in difficult change efforts, missed goals, increased costs, decreased customer service, and decreased quality. This is not to say that every organization is missing them. It is, however, a suggestion to carefully consider their importance and level of development before embarking upon complex organizational change.

Worksheets are provided to assist in developing structured approaches.

5 | Leading Change

"A leader is a person you will follow to a place you wouldn't go by yourself."
—Joel Barker, futurist

"Understand that people only listen to preaching; they emulate behavior."
—Max DePree, Herman Miller, Inc.

Granny was a change leader of sorts. She was the first girl in the county to join the suffragettes; she was the first to learn how to drive a Studebaker, and when others needed lessons on working the clutch they knew they could count on Granny for instruction. Granny could organize any event and make it a success. When someone would tell Granny she was a natural-born leader she'd laugh and say it was because she was the shortest girl in school and everybody had to follow her in line anyway.

But I'd say Granny was a leader because her confidence in herself and others made people comfortable and secure around her. You could always count on her to say and do the right thing all the time. And when Granny would look you in the eye and listen to you like you were the only boy on earth, you knew you'd follow her anywhere.

Armed with the proper information, understanding, and confidence, we can all become highly effective masters of change.

* * *

During periods of change the level of personal, organizational, and marketplace uncertainty is high. Without strong leadership, focus, action, optimism, organization, and flexibility, any hope of successful change will be dashed. This does not mean strong leadership in terms of power and force. It does mean leadership that offers clear and decisive direction or focus while maintaining sensitivity to the human implications of change.

A leader, according to the widely acclaimed authors Warren Bennis and Burt Nanus, is "one who commits people to action, who converts followers into leaders, and who may convert leaders into agents of change." The difference between management and leadership is that managers do things right, while leaders do the right things.

In any organization there is a need for managers, leaders, and followers. Is being a "change" leader different? Are there different skills required of change leaders? Is the role of a change leader different from a leader during other, more stable times?

THE CHANGE PROCESS

To become a change leader, you must understand the change process. First we'll consider specific roles during a process. Then we'll consider some traits that appear to be critical, yet not exhaustive, of those traits necessary to assist in leading change. Finally, we will consider the difference in leadership necessary for times of change and times of maintenance.

The Key Roles

Most change specialists define four key roles that exist in the change process: the change sponsor, the change agent, the change target, and the change advocate.

The Change Sponsor

The first necessary role is that of the change sponsor, the individual or group that is responsible for legitimizing the change and giving it the necessary resources for implementation.

There are two types of sponsors. The first is the **Initial Sponsor**. This is the person or group who initially gives legitimacy and resources to the change. They approve the concept for someone or some other group to provide ongoing support. Frequently this occurs at the senior-most levels of the organization—e.g., Executive Committee, board, etc. The time of their active involvement is very short. It does not mean that they are not genuinely interested or supportive; it just means that they delegate ongoing sponsorship to the second type of sponsor—the Sustaining Sponsor.

As its name implies, the **Sustaining Sponsor** is the individual or group responsible for providing on-going legitimacy and resources to the change effort. This is the group that approves the ongoing budget, removes blocks/barriers, continues to demonstrate the importance of the project, among many other roles. The involvement of the sustaining sponsor is ongoing throughout the project. It must be maintained. It must be visible. Without the support of a sustaining sponsor, the project is likely to lose momentum and fail.

The Change Agent

The second role in the change process is that of the Change Agent. This is the person or group that is responsible for implementing the change. While they may be able to sponsor the change through a cascading effect in some portion of the organization, change agentship is a clearly distinct role. It is essential for success. The role of the agent is to "make it happen." Change Agents can be thought of as leaders/managers. To become an effective change agent and change leader...

- Understand your style of thinking and the styles of those you are leading and how to communicate with one another
- Surround yourself with a mix of styles to bring different perspectives to the table and use them openly and with enthusiasm
- Communicate, communicate, communicate
- Understand and accept the changes
- Recognize and reward behavior that supports the change and address those behaviors that do not
- Provide mutual support to other change agents
- Publicly and privately support the changes
- Challenge others in order to offer improvements
- Learn and grow from the process
- Deal with your own stress issues arising from the change experience, i.e., take care of yourself
- Support down, challenge up
- Take ownership
- Make offers and don't wait to be asked to do something

The Change Target

The third role is the Change Target. These are the individuals or groups that are required to change. These individuals or groups may be either internal or external to the organization. Examples include employees, vendors, customers, regulators, the community, etc.

Remember that the first part of the word "organization" is "organ" and the smallest component of the organ in this case is the individual. Each of these targets, despite the fact that they are part of a larger group, is an individual. Therefore, the role of the change agents is to address individual, specific, unique needs and responses to change, which make this role critical to success.

The Change Advocate

The fourth and final role, that of change advocates, is recognized in the change process.

A change advocate is a person or group that would like to create or change, but does not hold the power to legitimize it or allocate resources. The advocate simply advocates the change. The change advocate must "recruit" a sponsor to provide the necessary support for the desired change. Having an effective advocate is a powerful leadership role for the change, however; advocates are not necessary for each change. This role is necessary only if the initiating sponsor is not the creator of the change concept.

CHARACTERISTICS OF CHANGE LEADERS

We will limit ourselves to the characteristics of change leaders and not focus, for example, on characteristics of the change target.

Is there a separate set of characteristics for change leaders and leaders during less turbulent times? **NO**. The characteristics and traits are similar. The right leadership approach is necessary at all times; however, the situations with individuals and organizations (culture) and events (e.g., mergers, acquisitions, downsizings, etc.) require different experiences and the application of different skill sets. Therefore, is it correct to assume that a leader in one organization or one situation is best suited for all others? The answer is **NO**. Are there some characteristics that might serve a leader well during almost any change environment? The answer is **YES**. The difference is the situation.

Core Success Traits for Change Leaders

Here are some of the core skills, experiences, and characteristics of change leaders which we'll call "Success Traits for Change Leaders."

- Understanding of and deep commitment to the changes being undertaken
- Ability to listen to what others are saying as well as not saying. This will allow you to hear all that is being communicated. It also includes hearing with your eyes, ears and gut. Yes, using your intuition
- Ability to define a focus (vision) and stay with it. At the same time, you must remain open to altering the plans as events and circumstances change and more information is obtained
- Understanding all the implications of decisions and their impact on people and then making appropriate changes in plans
- Ability to think strategically and tactically
- Being well organized and helping others stay organized
- Sense of reality about the changes. Realize that there will be negative consequences as well as positive ones
- Ability to communicate the focus, the plan, the successes, and the realities of the change. It is essential that this communication come in many forms, at many times

- Ability to identify the rewards and the negative implications of the change
- Respect, faith, and trust in those around you. And that those around you have respect, faith, and trust in you
- Get others involved. Use the synergistic effects of participation and shared ownership

Commitment to Change

Max DePree, former Chairman of Herman Miller, Inc., offers some rather impressive characteristics for commitment in his book, *Leadership Jazz*. Here is a partial list of ideas and guidelines offered by DePree to help leaders approach the process of creative work:

- A leader protects unusual persons from the bureaucracy and legalism so ensconced in our organizations.
- A leader remains vulnerable to real surprise and to true quality.
- A leader works with creative people without fear.
- While respecting them, a leader is wary of incremental changes.
- A leader does not demand unreasonable personal or corporate loyalty.
- A leader arranges for projects to proceed along a narrowing path.
- A leader paves the way for change.
- A leader sets the example for openness and imagination and acceptance.
- A leader knows that the organization must understand how important it is to meet unmet needs.

Maggie was a good student. She understood the need for focus and organization during change. She put all her accumulated knowledge about change to work and developed a highly organized, focused change action plan. Her understanding of the Change Style Indicator and Herrmann Brain Dominance Inventory helped her organize her team and enabled them to function at their highest potential. They came up with three outstanding ideas to improve productivity and increase sales. With everyone on the same wavelength and change plans in hand, the team was ready to implement their agenda.

"So, Maggie, what's the problem," I asked.

"Money. People. Time. There aren't any resources allocated to this project, John," she said with exasperation. "Not a penny. Not a soul. Nothing. We worked for months to develop this whole project, and nothing! We're all fighting for the same resources—manufacturing, production, information services, sales—it's crazy. The President wants it all done—yesterday—but there's no support from the top. "

"Well, Maggie, this happens quite frequently in the companies I work with. Change comes so quickly and there is so much to be done, there isn't time to think, and some management just can't say no, so suddenly everyone is scrambling to do something, anything and nothing gets done. Someone's got to take the bull by the horns," I said. "Somebody's got to take charge. I can offer you a plan to present to management to help them focus on their priorities so that they can re-allocate resources effectively."

"Oh John, you don't mean me, do you?" Maggie said in a resigned voice. "Okay. You've gotten me this far, I may as well go for broke."

✳ ✳ ✳

Preparing for Change

One of the more difficult tasks during a period of change is to focus the organizational resources. During change, the competition for resources increases. The demands for resources by the change effort begin taking valued resources away from ongoing operations and other highly desirable activities. It is necessary for a change leader to be ready to take a global view and redirect resources while understanding that other key parts of the organization will suffer and reduce its capacities.

Considering that the natural resistance to change calls for resources to be held to maintain the status quo, someone must take responsibility for resource distribution and communication of the resource distribution and articulate his/her decision effectively.

As individuals and organizations we can only absorb so much change and so much activity. In his book, *Future Shock*, Alex Toffler defined "future shock" as the point at which the demands placed upon us are greater than our capacity to cope. Stan Davis and Christopher Meyer describe a similar phenomenon when the speed of complex change comes so rapidly that it becomes "a blur." Events begin to merge together and are not easily discernible.

Corporate meltdown is not a pretty sight. I was called in to help a company that was trying to implement too many changes at one time. These were major changes. Changes that would affect just about every single person in a company of 2,000 employees. The words "no," "can't", and "won't" didn't exist in the corporate culture. At the time I stepped in, there were thirty "hot" changes in various stages in a company that had never successfully changed in the past, and that consistently missed deadlines. Resources were bottle necked, employees were burned out, and the infrastructure was falling apart.

My challenge was to bring focus to the management at the company's senior executive level. After dividing the change areas into six categories and selecting change groups, we proceeded to set business imperatives by determining who's affected, what resources are being applied to this project, who's responsible for seeing the project through, what are the consequences if the project doesn't get done, and what are the recommendations for action. The imperatives were then taken to the chief executive officer for approval.

The exercise was very effective and quickly put the entire picture into focus so that the company could begin moving forward again.

Business imperatives are those critical tasks that support the mission and strategic goals. They do not include the "should do" items—only the "must do" items. The process outlined in Appendix D, on page 99, is designed to help leaders focus those priorities to include only the mission-critical items. By doing so, resources can be redeployed to support the essential priorities.

THE IMPORTANCE OF TIME MANAGEMENT

Time management can become a tremendous challenge during periods of change. While there are many excellent approaches to managing one's time, I recommend the approach provided by Stephen Covey in his book, *The 7 Habits of Highly Effective People*.

People effectively use the time management matrix (Appendix E, on pages 102 and 103) to identify how they are spending their personal, team and organizational resources of time. From this analysis, they have been able to re-allocate their efforts to more effectively and more efficiently support the goals they seek to achieve.

✳ ✳ ✳

A strong leader is a strong leader whether in the midst of change or on a normal business day. A strong change leader understands the various roles of the change process and the human aspects of change. Instrumental roles in the change process are change sponsor, change agent, change target, and change advocate. A strong change leader realizes that change leadership is situational and acts accordingly. The change leader makes a commitment to change and makes certain the organization is prepared for change. To become an effective change leader, you must lead the change by selecting the proper business imperatives and managing your time accordingly.

6 | Teamwork

"The most exciting breakthroughs of the 21st century will occur not because of technology but because of an expanding concept of what it means to be human."
—John Naisbitt & Patricia Aburdene

Granny and her friends were perfect examples of teamwork in action. They'd quilt together. They'd put up tomatoes together. For hours these ladies worked together, day in and day out, and everything just magically got done. Everyone had a task they did without effort. I never actually saw it happens, but the quilt squares got cut. Then they were sewn. Someone tied the knots, and someone else finished them off. And one day, just like that, the quilt was finished. Another one was started. It was seamless.

Then the tomatoes were picked. They were boiled. The jars were cleaned. The lids were put on. The jars were put up. And then we picked green beans. Everything just came together. Everybody knew what the next person would do. It was just like watching the tides roll in and out. After awhile you didn't even realize the tides were moving because you're kind of moving with them. Everyone knew her role in the process. If there was a problem, everyone stopped to help. Then it started all over again.

And I found myself in the middle of it all, just doing it. Doing work and enjoying it. Feeling like I was an important part of something special. The perfect team.

✳ ✳ ✳

Throughout this book, we have acknowledged that the world is changing, the workforce is changing, the marketplace is changing, and organizations are changing. How are these changes affecting our methods of performing our jobs or doing work?

In his book, *Cross-Functional Teams*, Glenn Parker says, "Individualism is out, teamwork is in. Specialization is out; a new style of generalism is in. Rigid organizational lines are out; fluid collaboration is in; power is out, empowerment is in. Hierarchical organizations are out, replaced by network organizations, adaptive organizations, informal organizations, and horizontal organizations. Right smack in the middle of all this sit cross-functional teams composed of experts ready to move quickly and flexibly to adapt to changing business needs."

Most of us have been on a team. Maybe it was a baseball, basketball, or swim team. Maybe it was a crisis team. Maybe it was a fund raising team for a charity. Maybe it was a new product development team.

What is a team? How is it different from a group? And are all teams alike?

WHAT IS A TEAM?

There are many definitions of a team. Here are a few that reflect the key components of a good team.

"A team is a group of people with a high degree of interdependence, geared toward the achievement of a goal or the completion of a task," according to Parker.

Katzenbach and Smith write, "A team is a small number of people with complementary skills who are committed to a common purpose, performance goals, and approach for which they hold themselves mutually accountable."

Teams versus groups

A group of people is a number of persons having in common certain characteristics or interests but having no overarching goal for which all are accountable. A team, on the other hand, is a group of interdependent people committed to achieving a goal by working together.

Types of teams in the corporate environment

While there are many forms of corporate teams, selecting the right type of team for the goal is critical to success. It is not the intent to provide an exhaustive description of the many types of teams and their appropriate uses; however, here is an example of the types of teams found in the workplace today:

- Organizational Policy-Making Teams (multi-functional)
- Task-Force or Cross-Functional Teams
- Department Improvement (functional)
- Quality Circles
- Self-Directed Work Teams (functional)
- Self-Managed Teams (functional)

In brief, functional teams are made up of a boss and his/her direct reports. A self-directed team is responsible for getting their work done and managing themselves. A cross-functional or multi-disciplinary team is comprised of people from different departments with a number of different disciplines and skill sets that no single individual possesses.

Although a self-directed work team approach is highly effectively, proceed with caution if the team members are inexperienced at managing large–scale, complex change.

THE IMPORTANCE OF TEAMS

In the era of downsizing, re-engineering, and flattening management levels, teams have become a highly effective solution to productivity problems created by fewer workers facing the same amount or increased workloads. The advantages are numerous and include:

- People like to associate with others
- Increased likelihood for synergistic results
- Increased productivity
- Effective delegation
- Increased "buy-in"
- Increased communication
- Focus the direction and quality of top-down leadership
- Foster new behaviors
- Facilitate cross-functional activities
- Enhanced organizational learning
- Single point of contact for information and decisions
- Improved complex problem solving
- Accountability to one another, as well as to management

A training magazine survey reports that employees and managers alike believe that teams have produced significant improvements in organizations:

- 76% said teams have improved employee morale
- 90% agreed that teams have improved the quality of products and services
- 85% said that teams have improved the level of customer service
- 81% felt teams have improved productivity

Teams not only work; they help create the relationship that's necessary to resiliency. Teams help promote communication between departments during this crucial time. If two heads are better when it comes to solving a problem, then a team can't lose.

Helping Teams Function Well

It is recommended that as much as possible be done to support teamwork and to foster an operating culture of teams. For this to happen much is required from organizational leaders, team members, and non–member colleagues. For teams to function well they need:

- Clear authority, responsibility, and expectations
- Time, money, knowledge, and human resources
- Visible acts of support
- Guidance
- Patience and understanding
- Orientation
- Selection of the best people possible for the team

Selecting team members

Selecting the best people for the task (or team) is crucial. The reality of organizational life is that in some instances the right person cannot participate or, because of political circumstances, is not allowed to participate. In other cases, the right person may not be identified for participation. Therefore, the team should be composed of the best people available. And, in making your selection, keep in mind that the team members must quickly gel in order to be as productive as possible. The following criteria should be considered when selecting people for participation on a team:

- Knowledge/expertise
- Availability
- Interest in the task/goal
- Ability to work as a team member (see list of team behaviors that follows)
- Desires personal and professional growth that may be derived from the experience
- Ability to adjust to the work demands of the team
- Ability to work with the other team members
- Ability to both take a leadership role and accept sublimation of ego

Glenn Parker's book, *Cross-Functional Teams Tool Kit, 1997*, provides an excellent example of how one might assess potential team members for inclusion. This tool can also be used to provide feedback to team members following a team experience. Furthermore, the tool can be used to create a database for use when considering people for future team assignments.

Utilizing HBDI for effective team building

This is also the area where the Herrmann Brain Dominance Inventory comes into play. When developing an effective team, it is best to bring people of all brain quadrants— rational, experimental, sensitive, and safe-keeping—to the table. As a leader, remember that the different types of people who ask "who, what, why, and how" provide a "whole brain" collective approach to problem solving. Without equal representation on your team, results will tend to be skewed toward the predominant quadrant and effectiveness will diminish. Remember that, overall, a company is whole–brained and every quadrant of the company must be communicated with in order for change to occur throughout.

Take the example of an educational organization that was going through major changes with a new president. Of the three vice presidents making up the executive group, two were new. Part of their challenge was to implement a new vision with new leadership in an environment that had not seen leadership changes at the top in 25 years. The overall goal was to get the team together to implement a strategic plan that had been created two years earlier. The challenge was to develop effective communication between teams. This is where the HBDI came into play. (See Appendix A on pages 93 and 94 and refer once again to Appendices B and C on pages 94–97.

Implementing a series of exercises involving a room-sized HBDI model, we learned that the organization leadership was actually "whole–brained." "But we don't act this way," someone said and everyone began chiming in. They didn't understand why they don't relate, why they can't communicate, why there is such a struggle at the top of the organization, and so forth.

Upon analysis it appeared that their weakest area was in the "B" quadrant. What had been happening was that they were caught between a chief financial officer who was clearly "A" quadrant, a president who was fairly blue and significantly "D" quadrant, a VP for development that was "C" quadrant and "B" quadrant, and VP for academics affairs (the one that is leaving) that was also"C" quadrant and "B" quadrant.

Through the HBDI we discovered that the president wanted everybody to be happy but he was struggling with deciding on the right thing to do. He was like the man in the circus who has plates on sticks spinning in the air, trying not to let any fall. The president was running around generating all kinds of ideas without support or resources, and nothing was happening.

It also became clear that the new president was a risk-taker while the old president was very controlled. The new president was willing to let the plates fall, all he wanted was for people to try, to at least get things moving. The faculty, which was mostly red quadrant, wasn't accustomed to taking chances or being in control of their own destinies for that matter. They were stymied by the fear of failure.

Thanks to the HBDI, by the end of the day faculty and management were were able to communicate enough to build teams who were ready to move ahead and implement the strategic plans that had been on hold. They realized that "Look, we can do some things to help not only us as a group, but to help us work with others as an entire college community, and improve our effectiveness in managing, leading, and participating in the changes that are taking place." They were able to reach a consensus to focus on three areas that they would then take action on. They chartered teams to address those areas and they began working through the team process to produce the agreed upon results.

Overall, the key to effective teams is to select the best available individuals for the team while creating opportunities for growth.

Guide for Team Behaviors

In order to be effective players, team members have to know the rules of good sportsmanship. The following is a list of team member behaviors that can help to facilitate the most effective teamwork:

- Seek to resolve conflict
- Actively participate and be "totally present"
- Come prepared
- Assume various roles of responsibility as appropriate
- Seek to understand before seeking to be understood
- Be courteous, honest, and trusting
- Be flexible
- Follow the rules
- Criticize ideas, not people
- Build on the ideas of others
- Maintain confidentiality
- Stick to the agenda
- Make commitments and keep them
- Use humor when appropriate
- Respect the rights and feelings of others
- Freely share knowledge, expertise, and skills
- Deal directly with conflicts
- Bring any complaints about the team to the team and support efforts to resolve them
- Think creatively and help others do so
- Make sure work sessions and meetings end with a summary of work accomplished, tasks assigned, and future agenda items

✳ ✳ ✳

In her quest for resource allocation, Maggie discovered the value of cross-functional teams. By organizing efficient groups of employees who could enhance each other's abilities, Maggie was able to increase productivity and achieve results with the resources that were available to her.

One of the most important tools she discovered for developing effective teams was the team charter. The charter gave team members a common goal, gave them authority to perform their duties, and allowed them to take ownership of the process, knowing they would have the support and resources necessary.

TEAM CHARTER

A team charter can serve as the thread that holds the team together and gives the group an "official" common goal and stake in the process.

An excellent example of the effective use of a team charter was developed for a management group that had a tendency to jump right into a problem and solve it without calling on the whole brainpower of their organization. They would use their own people, involve too many, and miss the chance to make better decisions and focus clearly on what they wanted to do.

I first helped them decide on three areas that would move them forward. Then they worked together in groups to create a team charter for their groups. Then they worked to define what the teams would do and gave them a time line for completion. In essence through the charter, the managers gave up their ownership of the problem and allowed others to do their jobs.

I have frequently found that by having a team, or work group sponsor, complete the team charter found in Appendix F, on pages 104 and 105, they are able to create clear direction and authority for the team. In the absence of this type of initial support from the sponsor, the team can draft the charter and present it to the sponsor for approval. .

Team Members

Utilizing teams is one of the major changes taking place in business operations today. Teams have become a highly effective solution to productivity problems created by fewer workers facing the same or increased workloads. Teams share a common goal for which they are accountable. An effective change leader will choose the best available people for teams, provide them with behavior guidelines, and draw up a charter that will give the team direction. An effective team is made up of a "whole brain" which includes

67

rational people who determine what changes are needed, feeling people who think about the personal aspect of the change, risk-takers who will find a better way to implement the change, and the doers who will implement the change.

7 | Project and Action Planning

"It doesn't matter where you came from—it just matters where you're going."
—Barbara DeAngelis, Ph.D., author

"O.K. John," said Maggie, looking over her notes from the meetings of the past few months, "we're on our way. I can't believe it." She had gone through the entire process. Her team had its charter, its sponsor, and the okay from management to move on.

"I'm excited. Because it's all here and we're ready to go, but quite honestly I don't know where to go from here. Change is definitely frightening and I want to make sure I don't make any mistakes."

"Maggie, change isn't frightening. It's how people react to it that makes it that way. It's the fear of not knowing what to expect, of not knowing why things are happening, or when, or where, or how. You can lessen the fear by providing people with as much information as possible as you proceed. You are dealing with people, a human element. And you learned earlier that all people face change differently. Now that you know where you're headed, you've got to let others see the map and make sure they understand the directions. I've developed a change project framework for that purpose."

"Sounds logical," said Maggie. "Where do I start?"

"At the beginning. Why are you making this change in the first place?"

✳ ✳ ✳

In this chapter we will define a change project framework and provide an outline that will help you define your change projects. This outline focuses on the human aspects of change rather than the technical aspects of change.

Drawing from the information in the change project framework outline, we will be able to develop an action planning worksheet which focuses on the specific actions necessary for effective implementation.

These will later be linked to the communication efforts associated with change that are outlined in Chapter Eight.

THE CHANGE PROJECT FRAMEWORK

It is believed that projects that implement change are comprised of three basic components: rationale, process, and results (illustrated in Appendix G on page 107). While they are illustrated in a linear or progressive fashion, the results must be closely related to the rationale in order to insure success of the desired change.

Any journalism, communications, or public relations student will recognize the format of the change project framework as it closely resembles the five Ws of news reporting: who, what, when, where, why, and how. The answers to these 5 Ws are also the answers essential to effective implementation of the change project.

Rationale

Why are we changing? The rationale is defined as the reason for the change.

Process

The process includes how the change will occur, who is involved and affected, when the change will occur both in an overall fashion and in a step-by-step manner, and where the changes will occur—e.g., individuals, units, corporation-wide.

Results

The third element is the results. This includes what changes are desired. In other words, what will be different once the change has been implemented.

Note that the illustration shows each component with a pointed top. This is to reinforce that each component of the change must be developed based on the premise that individuals are involved and affected. Remember the importance of "What's in it for me," which was discussed in Chapter Two.

THE CHANGE PROJECT OUTLINE

During periods of rapid, large–scale, and complex change, it is important that change leaders and targets thoroughly understand the change project being undertaken.

The Change Project Outline found in Appendix H, on page 108, is intended to support the development and communication of the change. Change sponsors and/or change agents should complete this outline. It is essential that agreement on all aspects of the change projects is reached in order to facilitate understanding, commitment, and success. (See Appendix I, on page 112, for the Action Planning Worksheet.)

✳ ✳ ✳

When planning your change, remember to answer these questions and communicate the answers to everyone involved. Why is the change occurring? How will it occur? When will it happen? Where will it occur? Who will be involved and who will be affected? What will be the end result? Cover all the bases, but most of all, remember, the only thing most people really want to know is "what's in it for me?" and plan accordingly.

8 | Communicating Change

"The conversations we have drive the actions we take that lead to the results we achieve."
—**John L. Bennett**

I never realized how much influence Granny really did have on me until I wrote this book. She always read to me, and she would change her voice to suit every character. And I'd really have to listen, and listen hard, to be sure she didn't mix up the voices. She rarely did. Sometimes she'd make me repeat what she just said to be certain I was paying attention. And we always had to write letters to her when we were at home to tell her what were doing and to thank her. But what Granny did best was listen to me. She let me talk for hours on end. And I could tell her anything. I thought I was the most eloquent person in the world. She taught me early on that communication is the glue that held us all together. If family didn't tell each other what was going on, who would? The same holds true for companies. If we don't tell each other what's going on, who will?

✳ ✳ ✳

Suppose you threw a party and nobody came? Suppose you developed a change plan and nobody knew about it?

Among the leading reasons change efforts fail is a lack of proper and adequate communication. In your organization, during times of change, can you recall ever having heard anyone complain about receiving too much of the right information at the right time? I have never had anyone make such a comment. In fact, what we frequently hear are comments about the results of poor decisions, lack of teamwork, wasted efforts and resources, all resulting from a lack of good information when it was needed during the change.

In a 1998 survey of 480 companies and public organizations by the National Association of Colleges and Employers, communication abilities are ranked number one among personal qualities of college graduates sought by employers. Work experience and motivation were second and third (*The Wall Street Journal*, December 29, 1998).

During a one-year period, we surveyed 25 groups of employees in more than 15 organizations asking them questions about the potential problems that may arise during implementation of an upcoming complex change. Line employees, managers, and supervisors alike identify communication issues as the most frequent challenge. Poor communication was the most frequently cited potential problem by all employees.

THE HBDI COMMUNICATION FRAMEWORK

Once again, the Herrmann Brain Dominance Inventory (HBDI) provides an excellent model on which to build a communication framework.

As you are already aware, the HBDI is an instrument designed to self-identify thinking-style preferences. The assumption is that our thinking preferences influence interests and these interests lead us to engage in certain activities from which we can develop competence.

For example, a person interested in data and financial information is more likely to engage in accounting and finance professions and, thus, be more competent in those types of activities than someone less interested.

Another example: someone interested in spatial design and artistic expression is more likely to engage in graphic design activities. Each person is a coalition of several thinking styles. In other words, we have a variety of thinking preferences. Some are stronger than others, which leads to increased desire and competence in a particular area.

Remember that the Herrmann model defines four thinking styles. Each of the four thinking styles has its own strengths, and each thinking style has a preferred communication style. (See Appendix J, Expectations of the Listener, on page 114.)

Remember too, that a company as a unit is "whole brained" and it is up to you to communicate change in a manner which each style of thinker will understand.

An example of targeted communication involves a chief financial officer of an educational organization who operated very strongly from her "A" quadrant preference and the VP for academic affairs who operated in his equally strong "C" quadrant preference.

While she is handing him spreadsheets that are saying how horrible the financial situation of the college is, crying, "Fire, fire, the house is burning, and we better be doing something." He's taking all of her spreadsheets and literally throwing them in the trash. They mean nothing to him.

Keeping their different preferences in mind, we were able to advise the financial officer, Janine, in effective communication techniques. What was basically said was, "Brad needs you to sit down face-to-face with him, talk with him about what those numbers mean, and better yet, paint him pictures."

So, Janine and Brad started having regular meetings and she would explain what the numbers meant in his vocabulary. He started waking up to what he could do as the VP of Academic Affairs (with most of the college reporting to him) to start applying some solutions to the financial problem.

Remember that a company is made up of a number of different thinking types. You must reach the "whole brain" in the appropriate ways to effectively implement the desired change. From this we are able to link the framework for change project planning described in Chapter Two.

Communication Methods

You'll discover, as Maggie found, that because of the diverse human element involved, there is no one right way to communicate the plan to all employees.

After Maggie completed her change project framework worksheets, she could analyze who needed what kind of information and, by looking at the "whole brain" picture, the best ways to communicate the plan. She realized that she needed audio and visual presentations. She needed communications with different verbage to reach different audiences. She recognized that communication went beyond newsletters and flyers to video conferencing and telephone hot lines. The more bases she covered and the more diverse her delivery methods, the more likely she would reach the largest target.

There are many methods of communicating during times of change and non-change and the correct method is the one that works best for the receiver. Here are a few examples that worked for Maggie:

- Change project newsletters
- Face-to-face, one-on-one meetings
- Briefings
- Memos/letters
- Paycheck stuffers
- Bulletin boards—electronic and physical
- Training material
- Video tapes, CDs, and audio tapes
- Teleconferences
- Group meetings/briefings

- Posters, signs, bumper stickers, t-shirts
- Video conference
- Open time meetings in the break room
- Hot line to check out rumors
- Time limit on responding to questions

The key is to avoid getting so wrapped up in the changes that we forget to communicate with change sponsors, agents, and targets.

The 5 x 3 x 4= Ah Ha! Rule

A good guiding principle is to communicate each message to each audience at least five times in at least three different ways considering the four different thinking styles outlined above. If this seems like too much communication, keep in mind that each of us will process the change in a personal way. Also, remember that we are constantly bombarded with information throughout the course of the day that may interfere with our reception the first time around. Refer to the change responses outlined in Chapter Two.

People want different kinds of information in different forms and at different times. I call this the rule of 5 x 3 x 4 = Ah Ha! Therefore, developing a communication strategy for this period of change will help insure that the right information is getting to the right people, in the right format, and at the right time.

To help develop communication strategies use the following Communication Planning Worksheet. By referring to the change project outline in Chapter Seven, you will determine your target audiences. These can be identified from your list of sponsors, agents, and targets. (See Appendix K, Change Communication Action Plan Worksheet, on page 117.)

Once the communication strategies are drafted, it is recommended that you create a matrix similar to the example below to insure that overlapping strategies are coordinated and the strongest impact can be derived. In addition, this type of coordination will help prevent omissions and assist in maximizing resources.

COMMUNICATION PLANNING MATRIX
Messages and Audiences...
The Communication Plan

Once the strategy is developed, it is time to develop the actual plan. This book provides project/action planning worksheets to help you develop a thorough communication program, secure the necessary sponsorships, resources, etc., and to help you monitor and adjust the plan as it is implemented.

The overall communication plan might include such components as:

- Purpose of the plan
- Authorization
- Resource budget: human, financial, etc.
- Communication target audiences: change sponsors, agents, and targets
- Key messages
- Selected communication methods
- General and specific time frames
- Measures of success

* * *

The difference between the success and failure of a change effort is communication. No one ever complained that they had too much information at just the right time to be effective. When preparing communiqués, remember that people process information differently, so you should prepare a variety of communication materials accordingly. A good guiding principle is to communicate each message to each audience at least five times in at least three different ways considering the four different thinking styles outlined above, or 5 x 3 x 4=Ah Ha! Don't get so caught up in the change that you forget to communicate with your change sponsors, targets, and agents. And always remember to communicate, communicate, communicate!

IV

Time to Change

Well, there you have it. We can't avoid change but we can make it more palatable by knowing what it is and understanding how it affects us. There are three types of change: minor, significant, and traumatic. Minor changes or inconveniences practically take care of themselves with little or no effort. Significant changes take work and resources but they can be surmounted. Traumatic changes take strength, determination, and resources. Although sometimes they may seem overwhelming, we can and do make it through traumatic changes with planning.

We can look at change as a challenge, as an opportunity, or as a danger; it's up to us. With every change there's an ending and a beginning. It's the transition in between the stages that can get us stuck, because that's where we begin to question the logic of the change and that's when the fear of personal impact may appear. If we begin to question "What's in it for me?" we're reacting in a normal way and from this point we have our footing and we can begin our climb.

The bottom line is that change is everywhere

If you remember just one thing from this book, let it be this: We all react to change in our own way and at our own speed—this is the human aspect of change. Like death, divorce, or other great losses, change is the end of old ways and brings with it a period of grieving which is natural. Everyone mourns differently, for a different amount of time. We can't tell the widow or widower when it's time to move on. They must decide when the time is right, and it may not be exactly the timeframe we had in mind. We must accept this and act accordingly.

When we're in transition, between the old and the new, we will doubt our ability to make it, as well as our colleagues' abilities, but this will pass as we become more informed. We need to mourn the loss of old ways in order to make way for the new ones. But we don't all do it or accept it at the

79

same time, and some of us may never accept it no matter what. As a change leader it is vital to understand this discrepancy in response adjustment, otherwise you may think your efforts are failing when, in actuality, paradigms may just be shifting, some slower than others.

We can run but we cannot hide from change. However, if we are flexible and welcome change we will be able to make it through. We can increase our adaptability by increasing our capacity for change. We can take change and use it to our advantage or we can fight it. We can thrive or perish. It's our call.

Your capacity for resilience can be increased by strengthening your abilities to focus, to be proactive, to be positive, to be organized, and to be flexible. Start by being proactive and begin to work on strengthening these traits in your own life—today.

A strong leader is a strong leader whether in the midst of change or on a normal business day. A strong change leader understands the various roles of the change process and the human aspects of change. These roles are change sponsor, change agent, change target, and change advocate. A strong change leader realizes that change leadership is situational and acts accordingly. The change leader makes a commitment to change and makes certain the organization is prepared for change. To become an effective change leader you must lead the change by selecting the proper business imperatives and managing your time accordingly.

Utilizing teams is an example of one of the major changes taking place in business operations today. Teams have become a highly effective solution to productivity problems created by fewer workers facing the same amount of or increased workloads. Teams share a common goal for which they are accountable. An effective change leader will choose the best available people for teams, provide them with behavior guidelines, and draw up a charter that will give the team direction.

When planning your change, remember to answer the following questions and communicate the answers to everyone involved. Why is the change occurring? How will it occur? When will it happen? Where will it occur? Who will be involved and who will be affected? What will be the end result? Cover all the bases but, most of all, remember the only thing most people really want to know is "What's in it for me?"

The difference between success and failure in a change effort is communication. No one ever complained that they had too much information at just the right time to be effective. When preparing communiqués, remember that people process information differently so you should prepare a variety of communication materials accordingly. A good guiding principle is to communicate each message to each audience at least five times in at least three different ways considering the four different thinking styles outlined above or 5X 3X 4=Ah Ha!!! Don't get so caught up in the change that your forget to communicate with your change sponsors, targets, and agents.

And always remember to communicate, communicate, communicate.

Now it's your turn to lead the way.

EPILOGUE

"Maggie? It's John, do you have a minute?"

"Sure, John. What's up?"

"I'm having this communication problem with one of my clients. We're having a team problem. We did an HBDI on the management group and two members are in the "D" quadrant and three are in the "B" quadrant and one is in the "C" quadrant, and we're not getting anywhere. What do you think the problem is?"

"Well John, you know, when you observe the people in the HBDI quadrants at the seminars, you'll find that people who share the same quadrant talk with each other automatically. Then they'll talk to those next to them or to those in front of or behind them, but they rarely talk to the quadrant diagonal to them. Your whole team is diagonally challenged. I'm guessing that's because they don't speak the same language. The 'creatives' and the engineers. Pretty tricky. Maybe you'll have to use the "C" quadrant as the interpreter since he can converse in either direction. Perhaps he could be your communication leader."

"Maggie, that could work. Thanks. By the way, congratulations, Ms. Vice President of Marketing."

"You are very welcome, Mr. Bennett. Keep in touch."

BIBLIOGRAPHY AND RESOURCES

This list of references is intended to provide a broad spectrum of resources related to the topics discussed in this book. Many of the listings were not directly cited; however, they provided inspiration or background material. Some are included as references for professional and personal growth.

And, by no means is this list intended to include all available excellent resources on the topic. Search and discover; explore and experience; grow.

Nature and Response to Change

Barker, Joel Arthur. *Future Edge: Discovering the New Paradigms of Success.* New York: William Morrow and Company, Inc., 1992.

———. *Paradigms: The Business of Discovering the Future.* New York: Harper Business, 1992.

Bridges, William. *Managing Transitions: Making the Most of Change.* Reading, MA: Addison-Wesley, 1991.

Conner, Daryl R. *Managing at the Speed of Change: How Resilient Managers Succeed and Prosper Where Others Fail.* New York: Villard Books, 1992.

Covey, Stephen R. *The 7 Habits of Highly Effective People.* New York: Simon & Schuster, 1989.

Davis, Stan and Christopher Meyer. *Blur: The Speed of Change in the Connected Economy.* Reading, MA: Addison-Wesley, 1998.

Kantrow, Alan M. *The Constraints of Corporate Tradition: Doing the Correct Thing, Not Just What the Past Dictates.* New York: Harper & Row Publishers, 1987.

Kübler-Ross, Elisabeth. *On Death and Dying.* New York: Macmillan Publishing, 1969.

Miller, Lawrence M. *Barbarians to Bureaucrats: Corporate Life Cycle Strategies.* New York: Fawcett Columbine, 1989.

Musslewhite, W. Christopher and Robyn D. Ingram. *Change Style Indicator: Facilitator's Guide*. San Francisco: Josey-Bass Pfeiffer, 1998.

Osborn, Carol. *The Art of Resilience: 100 Paths to Wisdom and Strength in an Uncertain World*. New York: Three Rivers Press, 1997.

Pritchett, Price. *The Employee Handbook of New Work Habits for a Radically Changing World*. Dallas: Pritchett & Associates, Inc., 1994.

Pulley, Mary Lynn. *Losing Your Job—Reclaiming Your Soul*. San Francisco: Jossey-Bass Publishers, 1997.

Sheehy, Gail. *New Passages: Mapping Your Life Across Time*. New York: Random House, 1995.

Stoltz, Paul G., PhD. *Adversity Quotient: Turning Obstacles into Opportunities*. New York: John Wiley & Sons, Inc., 1997.

Weinberg, Gerald M. *The Secrets of Consulting: A Guide to Giving & Getting Advice Successfully*. New York: Dorset House Publishing, 1985.

ORGANIZATIONAL COMPONENTS
Leadership

Bennis, Warren and Burt Nanus. *Leaders: The Strategies for Taking Charge*. New York: Harper & Row Publishers, 1985.

Bethune, Gordon. *From Worst to First: Behind the Scenes of Continental's Remarkable Comeback*. New York: John Wiley & Sons, Inc., 1998.

Block, Peter. *The Empowered Manager*. San Francisco: Jossey-Bass Publishers, 1987.

Carter, Wendy. *Managing Organizational Change*. New York: McGraw-Hill, 1994.

Conner, Daryl R. *Leading at the Edge of Chaos*. New York: John Wiley & Sons, Inc., 1998.

DePree, Max. *Leadership is an Art*. New York: Dell Publishing, 1989.

DePree, Max. *Leadership Jazz*. New York: Dell Publishing, 1992.

Greenleaf, Robert K. Servant *Leadership: A Journey into the Nature of Legitimate Power and Greatness*. New York: Paulist Press, 1977.

Heider, John. *Tao of Leadership*. New York: Bantam, 1985.

Hersey, Paul. *The Situational Leader*. New York: Warner Books, 1984.

Kanter, Rosabeth Moss. *The Change Masters: Innovation & Entrepreneurship in the American Corporation*. New York: Simon & Schuster, 1983.

Katzenbach, Jon R. *Real Change Leaders: How You Can Create Growth and High Performance at Your Company*. New York: Random House, 1996.

Kissler, Gary D. *The Change Riders: Managing the Power of Change*. Reading, MA: Addison-Wesley, 1991.

Kuczmarski, Susan Smith and Thomas D. Kuczmarski. *Values-Based Leadership*. Prentice-Hall, 1995.

Nadler, David A. *Champions of Change: How CEOs and Their Companies are Mastering the Skills of Radical Change*. San Francisco: Jossey-Bass Publishers, 1998.

Senge, Peter M. *The Fifth Discipline: The Art & Practice of the Learning Organization*. Doubleday Currency, 1990.

Senge, Peter M., Charlotte Roberts, Richard Ross, Bryan Smith and Art Kleinger. *The Fifth Discipline Fieldbook*. New York: Doubleday Currency, 1994.

Schen, Edgar H. *Organizational Culture and Leadership,* Second Edition. San Francisco: Jossey-Bass Publishers, 1992.

Smith, Douglas K. *Taking Charge of Change: 10 Principles for Managing People and Performance*. Reading, MA: Addison-Wesley Publishing Company, 1996.

Tichy, Noel M. and Mary Anne Devanna. *The Transformational Leader*. New York: John Wiley & Sons, Inc., 1986.

Tregoe, Benjamin B., John W. Zimmerman, Ronald Smith and Peter M. Tobia. *Vision in Action: Putting A Winning Strategy to Work*. New York: Simon & Schuster, 1989.

Wilkins, Alan L. *Developing Corporate Character: How to Successfully Change an Organization Without Destroying It*. San Francisco: Jossey-Bass Publishers, 1989.

Teamwork

Gordon. "Work Teams: How Far Have They Come?" Training, October 1992, pp. 59-64.

Harrington-Mackin, Deborah. *The Team Building Tool Kit*. New York: Amacom, 1994.

Katzenbach, Jon R. and Douglas K. Smith. *The Wisdom of Teams: Creating the High-Performance Organization*. Harvard Business School Press, 1993.

Kayser, Thomas A. *Team Power: How to Unleash the Collaborative Genius of Work Teams*. Burr Ridge, IL: Irwin Professional Publishing, 1994.

Naibitt, John and Patricia Aburdene. *Megatrends 2000: Ten New Directions for the 1990's*. New York: William Morrow and Company, Inc., 1990.

Nadler, David L., Janet L. Spencer and Associates. *Executive Teams*. San Francisco: Jossey-Bass Publishers, 1998.

Parker, Glenn M. *Cross-Functional Teams*. San Francisco: Jossey-Bass Publishers, 1994.

Sherriton, Jacalyn and James L. Stern. *Corporate Culture/Team Culture: Removing the Hidden Barriers to Team Success*. New York: American Management Association, 1997.

Syer, John and Christopher Connolly. *How Teamwork Works: The Dynamics of Effective Team Development.* McGraw-Hill, 1996.

Project and Action Planning

Belanger, Thomas C. *Successful Project Management.* American Management Association, 1995.

Frame, J. Davidson. *Managing Projects in Organizations.* Jossey-Bass Publishers, 1995.

Greer, Michael. *The Project Manager's Partner: A Step-by-Step Guide to Project Management.* Amherst: HRD Press, Inc., 1996.

Martin, Paula and Karen Tate. *Project Management Memory Jogger: A Pocket Guide for Project Teams.* Methuen, MA: GOAL/QPC, 1997.

Project Management Institute. *A Guide to the Project Management Body of Knowledge.* 1996.

Wysocki, Robert, Robert Beck, Jr., and David B. Crane. *Effective Project Management: How to Plan, Manage, and Deliver Projects On Time and Within Budget.* New York: John Wiley & Sons, Inc, 1995.

Communicating Change

D'Aprix, Roger. *Communicating For Change: Connecting the Workplace with the Marketplace.* San Francisco: Jossey-Bass Publishers, 1996.

Harkins, Phil. *Powerful Conversations: How High-Impact Leaders Communicate.* New York: McGraw Hill, 1999.

Herrmann, Ned. *The Whole Brain Business Book.* New York: McGraw-Hill, 1996.

Larkin, T.J. and Sandra Larkin. *Communicating Change: Winning Employee Support for New Business Goals.* New York: McGraw-Hill, 1994.

Palmer, Parker J. *To Know as We Are Known: Education As a Spiritual Journey.* San Francisco: HarperSanFrancisco, 1993.

Others

DeAngelis, Barbara. *Real Moments.* New York: Dell Trade Paperback, 1994.

Forisha-Kovach, Barbara. *The Flexible Organization: A Unique New System for Organizational Effectiveness and Success.* Englewood Cliffs, NJ: ___, 1984.

Galpin, Timothy J. *The Human Side of Change: A Practical Guide to Organization Redesign.* San Francisco: Jossey-Bass Publishers, 1996.

Kilmann, Ralph H., Mary J. Saxton, Roy Serpa and Associates. *Gaining Control of the Corporate Culture.* San Francisco: Jossey-Bass Publishers, 1985.

Roberts, Cokie. *We Are Our Mothers' Daughters.* New York: William Morrow and Company, Inc., 1998.

Woodward, Harry and Steve Buchholz. *Aftershock: Helping People Through Corporate Change.* New York: John Wiley & Sons, Inc., 1987.

APPENDICES

A | Personal Change Action Plan

I (we) will develop our capacity for change by taking action to improve

_____.

I (we) will take the following specific actions. These are things that I (we) will start/stop doing or do more/do less of in order to develop resilience.

Start/Stop/Do More/Do Less	Specific Action	Target Date

A *UPPER LEFT*

- ☐ Gathering facts
- ☐ Analyzing issues
- ☐ Arguing rationally
- ☐ Forming theories
- ☐ Measuring precisely
- ☐ Problem solving logically
- ☐ Financial analysis and decision making
- ☐ Understanding technical elements
- ☐ Critical analysis
- ☐ Working with numbers, statistics, data and precision

- ☐ Finding overlooked flaws
- ☐ Approaching problems practically
- ☐ Standing firm on issues
- ☐ Maintain a standard of consistency
- ☐ Providing stable leadership and supervision
- ☐ Reading fine print in documents/contracts
- ☐ Organizing and keeping track of data
- ☐ Developing detailed plans and procedures
- ☐ Articulating plans in an orderly way
- ☐ Keeping financial records straight

B *LOWER LEFT*

B | Whole Brain Model

UPPER RIGHT **D**

- ☐ Reading the signs of coming change
- ☐ Seeing "the big picture"
- ☐ Recognizing new possibilities
- ☐ Tolerating ambiguity
- ☐ Integrating ideas & concepts
- ☐ Challenging established policies
- ☐ Synthesizing unlike elements into a new whole
- ☐ Inventing innovative solutions to problems
- ☐ Problem solving in intuitive ways
- ☐ Simultaneous processing of different input

- ☐ Recognizing interpersonal difficulties
- ☐ Anticipating how others will feel
- ☐ Intuitively understanding how others feel
- ☐ Picking up the non-verbal cues of interpersonal stress
- ☐ Engendering enthusiasm
- ☐ Persuading, conciliating
- ☐ Teaching
- ☐ Sharing
- ☐ Understanding emotional elements
- ☐ Considering values

LOWER RIGHT **C**

A

RATIONAL SELF

Analyzes
Quantifies
Is Logical
Is Critical
Is Realistic
Likes Numbers
Knows about Money
Knows how Things Work

Takes Preventive Action
Establishes Procedures
Gets Things Done
Is Reliable
Organizes
Is Neat
Timely
Plans

SAFEKEEPING SELF

B

C | OUR DIFFERENT SELVES

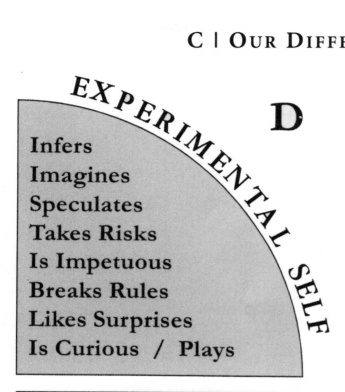

EXPERIMENTAL SELF

D

Infers
Imagines
Speculates
Takes Risks
Is Impetuous
Breaks Rules
Likes Surprises
Is Curious / Plays

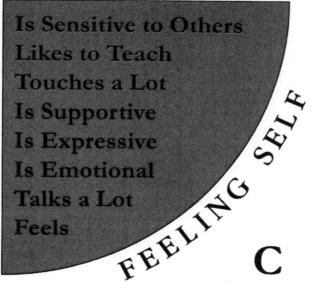

Is Sensitive to Others
Likes to Teach
Touches a Lot
Is Supportive
Is Expressive
Is Emotional
Talks a Lot
Feels

FEELING SELF

C

Reprinted by permission from Herrmann International   **97**

D | BUSINESS IMPERATIVES

ACTION STEPS TO SELECT BUSINESS IMPERATIVES:

Step 1: List all activities, projects, and perceived priorities for a work unit or organization for a specified future period.

Step 2: Agree upon a set of decision criterion—e.g., support strategic goals/objectives; resources are available; required by an outside body (customer, regulator, etc.).

Step 3: Complete the "Business Imperative Selection Worksheet."

Step 4: Compete the "Business Imperative Planning and Accountability Worksheet."

Step 5: Implement, monitor/control, and evaluate results.

BUSINESS IMPERATIVE SELECTION WORKSHEET

Possible Imperative	Relationship to Strategic Focus	Consequences of NOT Implementing	Business Imperative YES/NO

BUSINESS IMPERATIVE PLANNING AND ACCOUNTABILITY WORKSHEET

Business Imperative	Person Responsible	Sponsor	Implementation Date

Urgent

I
m
p
o
r
t
a
n
t

I
Activities: Crises, pressing problems, deadline-driven projects

N
O
T

I
m
p
o
r
t
a
n
t

III
Activities: Interruptions, some calls, some meetings, pressing matters, popular activities

Adapted from *The Seven Habits of Highly Effective People*, by Stephen R. Covey, 1989

E | TIME MANAGEMENT WORKSHEET

Not Urgent

II

Activities: Prevention, relationship building, planning, recreation

IV

Activities: Trivia, busy work, time wasters, pleasant activities

F | TEAM CHARTER

Team Name:

Sponsor:

Purpose of the Team:

Timeframe:

Stakeholder:

Desired Outcomes/Outputs/Deliverables:

Resources Needed/Assigned:

Contraints:

Team Skills/Expertise Needed:

Team Leader:

Team Members:

G | Change Project Framework

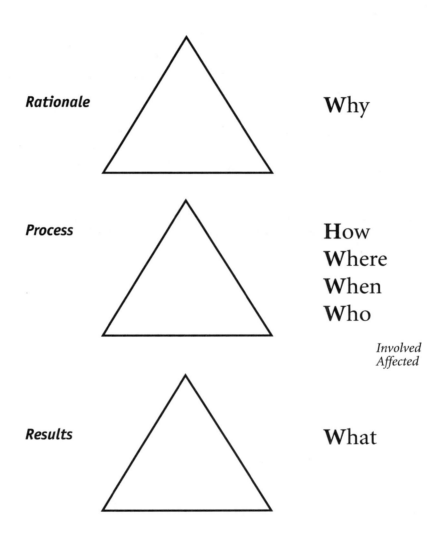

Rationale   **W**hy

Process   **H**ow
                               Where
                               When
                               Who

Involved
Affected

Results   **W**hat

H | Change Project Outline

Introduction

During periods of rapid, large–scale and complex change, it is important that change leaders and targets thoroughly understand the change project being undertaken.

The Change Project Outline is intended to support the development and communication of the change. Change sponsors and/or change agents should complete this outline. It is essential that agreement is reached in order to facilitate understanding, commitment, and success.

1. What is the change project being undertaken? Please write a brief description to thoroughly explain the change project.

2. What are the milestones or key components of the change project? These should include the key elements or achievements leading to successful implementation.

3. How will the success of this change project be measured? In other words, what are the critical measures of success?
Technical Measures:

Human Measures:

4. What are the financial, time, and other barriers, constraints, and/or "roadblocks" that might affect this project?
Financial:

Time:

Other Barrier/"Roadblocks":

5. What are the critical reasons driving the need/desire for this change?

Problem(s):

Opportunity(ies):

6. Why is the project important?

To the sponsor(s):

To the organization:

7. Who are the individuals and groups who will be affected by this change? In other words, who are the targets of this change?

8. How can the targets be made to see the desirability and accessibility of the change?

This change is desirable to the targets for the following reasons:

This change can be made accessible to the target by providing or eliminating the following:

9. What do you expect of the sponsor(s) of this change?

10. What are your responsibilities as a change agent?

I | Action Planning Worksheet

WHAT is the project being undertaken?

WHY is this action necessary?

WHO is involved, supportive, affected?

    Sponsors:

    Agents:

    Targets:
        Affected:

        Less Affected:

WHEN will this project/action plan begin and end?

WHERE will it take place?

HOW will the project be implemented?

Task (WHAT)	Responsible (WHO)	Deadline (WHEN)

A *UPPER LEFT* Reacts unemotionally.

Expects:

- ☐ Brief, clear & precise info
- ☐ Materials that are direct and to the point.
- ☐ Well articulated ideas presented in a logical format.
- ☐ Data and fact-based charts.
- ☐ Technical accuracy.
- ☐ Presentation in alignment with corporate goals & objectives.

Appreciates:

Wants precise facts

- ☐ *Critical Analysis*
- ☐ *A good debate*
- ☐ *Efforts to spend time wisely*

"WHAT?"

Expects:

- ☐ Step-by-Step unfolding of the topic.
- ☐ A written schedule & action plan.
- ☐ Thorough, timely and reliable follow through.
- ☐ Consistency
- ☐ Alignment with well established procedures.
- ☐ Assurance that this has been done before.
- ☐ Explanation of how it will happen
- ☐ References and background info

Appreciates:

Requires neatness and punctuality

- ☐ *Very low risk*
- ☐ *A written communication before session*
- ☐ *Proof that the "homework" has been thorough*
- ☐ *A scheduled appointment*

Reacts cautiously. "HOW?"

B *LOWER LEFT*

J | EXPECTATIONS OF THE LISTENER

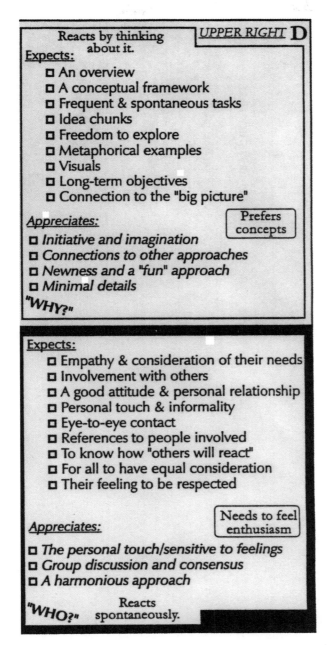

Reacts by thinking about it. **UPPER RIGHT D**

Expects:

- ☐ An overview
- ☐ A conceptual framework
- ☐ Frequent & spontaneous tasks
- ☐ Idea chunks
- ☐ Freedom to explore
- ☐ Metaphorical examples
- ☐ Visuals
- ☐ Long-term objectives
- ☐ Connection to the "big picture"

Appreciates:

Prefers concepts

- ☐ *Initiative and imagination*
- ☐ *Connections to other approaches*
- ☐ *Newness and a "fun" approach*
- ☐ *Minimal details*

"WHY?"

Expects:

- ☐ Empathy & consideration of their needs
- ☐ Involvement with others
- ☐ A good attitude & personal relationship
- ☐ Personal touch & informality
- ☐ Eye-to-eye contact
- ☐ References to people involved
- ☐ To know how "others will react"
- ☐ For all to have equal consideration
- ☐ Their feeling to be respected

Needs to feel enthusiasm

Appreciates:

- ☐ *The personal touch/sensitive to feelings*
- ☐ *Group discussion and consensus*
- ☐ *A harmonious approach*

"WHO?" Reacts spontaneously.

Reprinted by permission from Herrmann International **115**

K | CHANGE COMMUNICATION ACTION PLAN

Target	Messages	Methods	When	Responsible

ABOUT THE AUTHOR

John Bennett, MPA, is president of Lawton & Associates, an organizational development consulting firm committed to helping individuals and organizations achieve desired results through strategic and tactical approaches to coping with and improving from change. For more than 20 years he has been helping individuals and organizations prepare for, excel through, and improve from change.

As a professional speaker, John has educated while entertaining audiences on topics related to building resilience and leading change. As a consultant, he has worked with leading biomedical companies, human service organizations, professional associations, government agencies, and educational enterprises in developing capacities for successful adaptation. As a master trainer, he has helped thousands of people increase their ability and willingness to engage in change.

Prior to forming Lawton & Associates, John was CEO of a 23 million dollar American Red Cross biomedical services division. He has led pharmaceutical manufacturing and distribution operations as well as the development and delivery of essential human services. John has led mergers and turn arounds as well as new product development/marketing and computer system designs/installations.

John is a member of the National Speakers Association, the American Society for Training and Development, and the Institute for Management Consultants.

He lives on Lake Norman, in North Carolina, and travels extensively speaking, training, consulting, and coaching with domestic and international clients.

John would enjoy hearing from you through www.Lawton-Assoc.com or 1-877-8LAWTON.

John Bennett can be reached for keynote speeches, seminars, and professional coaching through:

Lawton & Associates
~~1-877-LAWTON~~
Lawtonbenn@aol.com

To order additional copies of *Leading the Edge of Change* contact:

Paw Print Press
PO Box 3816
Mooresville, NC 28117-3816

Please send me _____ copies ($11.95 each) plus $2^{50} shipping/handling per order. Contact Paw Print Press for volume discount pricing.

Credit Card Number _____ Expiration _____

Signature _____

Mailing address _____

City _____ State _____ Zip Code _____

Also available at your favorite bookstore. Price subject to change without notice.